SPURS WRITERS' CLUB

NMG

An NMG Publishing publication

© Norman Giller 2012

First published in 2012 by NMG Publishing

Ferndown, BH22 8XT

10 9 8 7 6 5 4 3 2 1

A CIP catalogue for this title is available from the British Library

ISBN 978-0-9567711-9-3

Typeset and designed by NMG Publishing, Dorset, UK

Printed and bound in the United Kingdom by
CPI Group (UK) Ltd, Croydon, CR0 4YY

Illustrations © 2012 Art Turner

TOTTENHAM
The Glory-Glory Game

SPURS WRITERS' CLUB

Devised and Edited
By **Norman Giller**
with contributions from a
parade of Spurs writers

Illustrations: **ART TURNER**

NMG

Art Turner
2011

Dedicated to the memory of
Bill Nicholson OBE

He managed with great dignity and style
Producing teams that played with a smile,
He's the man who put the heart into Spurs;
At White Hart Lane his spirit always stirs

CONTENTS 1

CONTENTS 2

SPURS WRITERS' CLUB

THE KICK-OFF By Norman Giller

WELCOME to the first book written as a mass anthem of acclaim to Tottenham Hotspur by the 2012-formed Spurs Writers' Club. Our members come in all shapes and sizes, jobs and professions, ages and gender, all of us with the common denominator of being imbued with the spirit of Spurs.

As you will discover in the following pages, our passion is your passion, our memories your memories, our rollercoaster experiences following the ups and downs of Tottenham the same dizzily unpredictable path that you have followed. And we all have the scars, the scares and the souvenirs to prove it.

When I called for volunteers to become founder members of the club on my Facebook and Twitter platforms, I was inundated with requests to take part. I had to restrict the first cut-off point to 45, and then set up an Associate Members wing for those prepared to support us in our first publishing project. And here we are, with *Tottenham, the Glory-Glory Game*.

The theme I chose for our first book is something we have all experienced, that first moment when you realised that Tottenham was YOUR team, that there could be no other, for richer for poorer, in sickness and in health, 'til death us do part. If there is any person who has any cause or just impediment why we should not be joined together in a form of matrimony, then you are to declare it now or forever hold your Ps and Qs.

Okay, so I am going a wee bit over the top with my marriage vows metaphor, but those with true love for Tottenham will know that it really is something like a betrothal ... and divorce is not recognised or even an option. To borrow from Kipling, we meet with triumph and disaster and treat those two imposters just the same.

Our members come from all walks of life. Among us we have a headmaster, a lawyer, several authors, a former Scotland Yard detective, a jazz entrepreneur, civil servants, company directors, three female members, a quadriplegic and a column of bright young journalists starting out on the sportswriting path. They come from far and wide and from around the corner, from Canada, the United States, Australia, New Zealand, Holland, Edmonton and Enfield.

The aims of our club are to write books together about Tottenham Hotspur that are informative, entertaining, from the heart and responsible, revealing and respectful – the sort of books that WE would like to read about what we consider the greatest club in the land.

With apologies, a little trumpet blowing about myself to lay down my marker for founding

Greavsie and Gilly ... no not Alan Gilzean but that's me on the left, Norman Giller. Greavsie and I have been pals for more than 50 years and he has been trying to shake me off in all that time, but the fact that we have written 20 books together proves he has failed. He was without any shadow of doubt the greatest goalscorer ever to wear a Spurs or England shirt. Anybody of a certain age is virtually guaranteed to have him in their dream Spurs team. He scored a record 357 First Division goals, including a club record 220 for Tottenham. Oh yes, and 44 goals in 57 England games. When I told Jimmy I was planning to form a Spurs Writers' Club he said: "You must be blankety-blank mad. Surely it would make more sense to form a Spurs Readers' Club." It's a funny old game.

the club. I have to date had 93 books published, including 20 in harness with Spurs legend Jimmy Greaves and several exclusively about Tottenham, such as the acclaimed *Lane of Dreams*, *The Golden Double* and *The Managing Game*. I also scripted the first ever official VHS video on the club in its Centenary year of 1982: *100 Years of Spurs,* which was presented by Greavsie and 30 years on is now considered a collectors' item, or even an antique.

During a long Fleet Street reporting and sub-editing career, including ten years as chief football writer for the *Daily Express*, I kept to strict press box neutrality, but I have been able to come out of the closet as a Spurs fan since surrendering most newspaper connections. My *Express* newspaper colleagues included the one and only Danny Blanchflower, from whom I drained every anecdote possible. This was not so difficult, because the verbose Danny Boy dripped stories like a running tap.

I counted legends like 'Sir' Bill Nicholson, Arthur Rowe and Sir Alf Ramsey as friends beyond the usual reporting relationship, Steve Perryman remains a good mate and Harry Redknapp and I used to stand shoulder-to-shoulder in Bobby Moore's drinking school at the Black Lion in Plaistow after home West Ham matches.

Friends of mine in the publishing business questioned my sanity when I told them of my Spurs Writers' Club plan. They considered it unworkable, pulling together 45 strangers, many of whom had never been published before, and getting them to meet deadline and content commitments. But the evidence is here in your hands that it *does* work. There are as many writing styles in this book as there are members of our club, and each and every one has risen to the occasion in their own way. I have edited gently, never dictating, quietly directing and drawing exactly the sort of memories I knew would make this a book rich in nostalgia and must reading for anybody with Tottenham in their soul.

I considered giving away Kleenex tissue with each copy of this *Glory-Glory Game*, because as you will discover there will be plenty of times when tears will be close. We like to think of it as the Tottenham book on which you can warm your hands with the true spirit of Spurs. It deserves to be on sale at the Spurs stores, but they have their own exclusive publishing club into which we would like to be invited. So most of our sales have to be on line.

After my kick-off chapter, we present the memories in age order – from a 75 year old all the way down to an 18-year-old journalism student who takes a fresh and very creative look at a well-trodden Tottenham trail. The illustrations are by my life-long friend Art Turner, the pen name of an artist who has been drawing a wage from Fleet Street newspapers across five decades. As you will see, he still has lead in his pencil and he captures a gallery of great Tottenham players.

Thank you for joining our publishing adventure, and look out for our next book in this Spurs Writers' Club series. Writers are redundant without readers. Please tell anybody you know with Tottenham tendencies to support our project.

Now, eyes down for the Glory-Glory Game ...

NORMAN GILLER
Occupation: Author/Publisher
Age: 71
Location: Dorset via London
Spurs fan since: 1950-51
All-time favourite player: Jimmy Greaves
Website: www.normangillerbooks.com
Blog: www.sportsjournalists.co.uk
Norman is the founder of the Spurs Writers' Club. A former chief football writer of the *Daily Express,* he is a sports historian who has had 92 previous books published, 20 0f them in harness with Lane legend Jimmy Greaves.

THE classic opening words to *The Go Between* by novelist L. P. (Leslie) Hartley are captured perfectly by the whirling world of football: "The past is a foreign country ... they do things differently there."

Come with me back to 1950-51. The place The Valley, the match Charlton Athletic v. Tottenham Hotspur, and there I was – a skinny as a pipe cleaner ten-year-old primary schoolboy in my older brother's hand-me-down short trousers – trembling wih excitement and anticipation of my first view of First Division football. I had been taken south of the Thames from my East End home by my Uncle Roy Robinson, who was expecting to convert me to his religion of worshipping Charlton.

It was a different game then, not just another country but another planet. Rationbook times, London still being rebuilt after the Second World War blitz, footballers earning £11 a week, going to and from the ground like the rest of us by bus and speaking a language that would be foreign to today's players.

There were wing-halves, inside-forwards, shoulder-charging and barging of goalkeepers, tackling from behind, two points for a win, no floodlights, no yellow and red cards, no TV cameras, a leather and laced panelled ball that was like a pudding on heavy, mud-heap pitches that made every step a challenge.

This trip to The Valley of dreams cost my Uncle three shillings (45p), two bob for him and a shilling for me to stand on the vast, concrete terracing behind the goal at the Floyd Road end of the sprawling stadium. There were 62,000 spectators shoehorned into the ground, and I could not see a thing through the heaving wall of fans towering above me.

No problem. Dock worker Uncle Roy picked me up as if I was a packing case and handed me high to the man in front, and I was carried – the stench of Weights and Woodbines in my nostrils – on a willing relay of raised hands above hundreds of heads, most adorned with flat caps, and down to a cramped standing place against the fence, right behind the goal being defended by Tottenham.

I will not pretend that sixty-plus years on I can remember the exact details of the match, but what has remained with me is the sense of excitement and the sheer ecstasy of feeling as if I was involved in the action. Yes, a spectator but I kicked every ball, scored goals that were missed and made every save. All these years later that sense of involvement in every game has never left me. I have been the Stanley Matthews, the Pele, the Bobby Charlton, the Greavsie, the Glenn Hoddle, the Ledley King of spectators. If only they would play the game the way I see it, my team would never lose

My Uncle Roy had been teaching me chants: "Come on you Robins ..." ... "Get in there you 'Addicks.'" He wanted me to wear a red and white rosette as big as my head, but instinct made me declare myself too shy to pin it to my jacket. Little did he know that I had been nobbled before he got to me by another uncle, Eddie Baldwin of Edmonton, who was my Godfather. He and my Aunt Emmy were Spurs through and through, and followed them home and away. The home bit was easy. They lived within the crowd's roar of White Hart Lane.

They had been filling my head and my imagination with stories of the great Tottenham teams, and telling me how they had waltzed away with the Second Division title in 1949-50 with what was known as Push and Run football. The cynics sneered that it was playground football that would be exposed in the top echelon of the First Division.

Now here I was immediately behind the goal at The Valley watching Arthur Rowe's Spurs chase and chastise Charlton with their push and run tactics that were simple yet sophisticated, predictable yet played to perfection. They followed the Arthur Rowe commandments: "When not in possession get into position ... make it simple, make it quick ... keep the ball on the ground ... the three As, accuracy, accuracy, accuracy ..."

There at right-back Alf 'The General' Ramsey was showing the poise and polish that made him a regular in the England team. Ahead of him right-half Billy (that's what they called him then) Nicholson was full of energy and urgency, making the team tick with his unselfish running and tigerish tackling. Striding across the pitch like a colossus was skipper Ronnie Burgess, as tough as if hewn from a Welsh mountain but able to intersperse delicate skill with his startling strength (no wonder Bill Nick once described him to me as the greatest player ever to pull on a Spurs shirt). Burgess would prompt the attack, and then in a blink of an eye be back at the heart of the defence helping out alongside immense centre-half Harry Clarke.

Imperious in the centre of the pitch was the thick-thighed emperor of the team, Eddie Baily, the 'Cheeky Chappie' of the dressing-room who could land a ball on a handkerchief from forty yards. He was the schemer in chief, providing a conveyor belt of telling passes for

Ted Ditchburn, a Superman of goalkeepers who flew into Norman Giller's heart

twin centre-forwards Len 'The Duke' Duquemin and Londoner Les Bennett. The Duke was a Channel Islander, the nearest thing to a 'foreigner' on the Spurs books.

Tottenham's alternative route to goal was down the wings, with flying Sonny Walters and tricky Les Medley turning defences inside out with their stunning running. Their crosses, usually to the far post, were met high and mightily by the Duke or Bennett, both of whom could head the ball as hard as I could kick it.

Incredibly, fifteen or so years later, I would be regularly interviewing Alf, Bill Nick, Ron Burgess and Eddie Baily in my role as chief football reporter for the *Daily Express*. Seeing them through my schoolboy eyes they were like giants, but one player stood above them all.

In about the tenth minute of the match, Charlton's powerchouse centre-forward Charlie Vaughan shook off a challenge from Harry Clarke and unleashed a thunderbolt shot from the edge of the Tottenham penalty area.

From my best view in the ground, I could see that the ball was going to fly into the top right hand corner of the net. Fifty thousand of the 62,000 crowd – Charlton fans – roared in anticipation of a goal and hundreds of wooden rattles produced an ear-shattering background effect like a snarl of snare drums.

Then out of nowhere appeared somebody doing a Superman impression. Was it a bird, was it a plane? No, it was the flying form of goalkeeper Ted Ditchburn, not touching the ball away like most goalkeepers would have tried to do. My schoolboy eyes looked on in amazement as he caught the ball while at full stretch and in mid-air.

It was a stunning, astonishing save that silenced everybody but the knot of 12,000 travelling Tottenham fans at the other end of the ground, who switched from cheering to choruses of the club theme song, McNamara's Band.

From that moment on I was a Tottenham disciple. It was love at first flight.

Throughout a long football reporting career I had to stick to press box neutrality, and it is not until recently surrendering newspaper work for full-time authorship that I have been able to come out of the closet as a Spurs supporter.

And I can trace the start of my love affair to that magical moment when Ted Ditchburn appeared to defy gravity and make a save that has lived on in my memory. Thank goodness there were no television action replays to taint or tarnish the picture in my head. It still sits there, and is occasionally brought out from the vaults of my memory and admired, without anybody being able to produce proof that perhaps, just perhaps, I have exaggerated the lightning shaft of genius that turned me into a lover of all things Lilywhite.

For the record, Tottenham forced a 1-1 draw thanks to an Alf Ramsey penalty and they pushed and ran their way to the League championship.

And a ten-year-old boy in his brother's hand me down short trousers went home to the East End converted to the Tottenham way of playing football.

It has been a long time coming, but at last I can apologise and say, "Sorry Uncle Roy."

BARRY HATCHER
Occupation: Jazz entrepreneur
Age: 75
Location: West Byfleet, Surrey
Spurs fan since: 1946
All-time favourite player: Jimmy Greaves

Barry is a hugely respected figure in the international jazz recording business, putting together top-flight musicians for classic sessions. He firmly believes he saw the best-ever Tottenham Hotspur ensembles who put the swing into Spurs.

MY memories of White Hart Lane started way back in 1946 when I was nine years old, following my Dad who had supported the Spurs since seeing them win the FA Cup in 1921. The strange thing was he was born and bred in South London, but supported a North London team (at least it wasn't the Arsenal!).

Although my Dad first took me to the Lane for the 1946/47 season, my first serious recollection of the joys of following the Spurs was the Push and Run team of 1950-51 managed by Arthur Rowe, which won Second and First Division titles in back-to-back seasons. The style of play was so simple and effective, but the team basically went into decline as the 50's went towards the 60's, because most of the players were veterans who served in the Second World War.

Then came the Glory-Glory Years with Bill Nicholson at the helm. A key man in the Push and Run ream, he assembled a squad that gave all fans (except those from Highbury) such pleasure. I clearly remember the arrival of Dave Mackay in March 1959, and when he first played I wondered what all the fuss was about as he looked rather ordinary. It transpired he was injured at Hearts (his previous club). and he promised the following season would be better when fully fit. How right he was! Around the same time John White joined, and I started to get the feeling the club was progressing towards being a pretty good side with the likes of Danny Blanchflower, Bobby Smith, and Cliff Jones etc.

There was a buzz of optimism about the approaching 1960-61 season, and with a bit of bad timing I missed the opening match because of the little matter of getting married and being on honeymoon. We watched with growing excitement as the team won the initial

11 League games and played a style of football that was out of this world.

All the home games were memorable for one reason or another, but if I had to choose a particular game that stands out in my memory it would be the match against Burnley on December 3 in front of 58000+ fans. At half-time Spurs were 4-0 up and coasting it. In the second-half Burnley – a magnificent team in those days, with players of the calibre of Jimmy Adamson and Jimmy McIlroy – produced the most amazing fight back I can ever remember. They scored four times to make the final score 4-4, with Spurs hanging on for dear life. Our nerves were shredded but we had been treated to a classic.

Spurs went on to win not only the League championship but also the FA Cup to become the first team of the 20rh Centiry to complete the 'impossible' Double.

The following season Jimmy Greaves was added to the team for £99,999, and I clearly remember his first game against Blackpool when he scored a hat-trick. His first goal – a scissors kick following a corner – was the stuff of dreams.

That season – 1961/2 – Spurs finished third in the League as well as retaining the FA Cup. Greavsie scored an exquisite goal after just 180 seconds to put them on the way to a 3-1 victory over their old Burnley rivals. This made up for the disappointment of a European Cup semi-final defeat by Benfica, when Jimmy had a perfectly good goal ruled off-side.

There were goals galore the following season when Spurs finished second, finding the net a remarkable 111 times – the last club ever to score over 100 goals in the old First Division. Even more memorable, they became the first English club to win a major European trophy by capturing the European Cup Winners' Cup.

Greavsie and little Terry Dyson – playing the game of his life – scored a couple of goals each in a 5-1 flattening of Atletico Madrid in Rotterdam. Remarkably, they did it without teak-tough talisman Dave Mackay, who failed a fitness test and was replaced by the assured Anglo-Italian Tony Marchi.

However, the outstanding game I remember from that season was on October 31 1962 against Glasgow Rangers, which was billed as the Championship of Great Britain. Spurs won 5-2 on an unforgettable night. I have never experienced such an atmosphere at any football before or since. It was a privilege to be in the crowd.

Sadly, the next few seasons were an anti-climax following the tragic death of John White, Danny's recurring knee injury and Dave Mackay breaking his leg twice. The heart and engine room of the team had been ripped out. Other players lost their form, and Bill Nicholson tried hard to restore the old magic by raiding the transfer market. But how do you replace genius?

Even my hero Jimmy Greaves went through a bad patch after being put in hospital for five weeks with jaundice in the autumn of 1965. This was during the build-up to the 1966 World Cup and Jimmy performed miracles to get himself fit for the tournament, only to

Terrt Dyson played the game of his life in the Cup Winners' Cup final

miss out on the final when left out by ex-Spur Alf Ramsey. It's a cruel old game.

Jimmy was never quite the same power after that attack of jaundice. He lost half a yard in pace, and in 1970 he was (heartbreaking for me) transferred to West Ham as part of the deal involving Martin Peters.

I just could not imagine Spurs without Greavsie, and as fate would have it his first game for West Ham the following season was at the Lane against Spurs. Needless to say, Jimmy scored and my Dad and I were so disillusioned we decided to sell our season tickets (for £18 each, having deducted 18 shillings for the West Ham match). The guy who sat next to us bought them.

We went back to the Lane the following season for one final game, which was Greavsie's testimonial match against Feyenoord. and yet again Jimmy scored.

This was was the end of our days at the Lane as both my Dad and I had lost interest in football because we disliked the crowd hooliganism and later the galloping greed and the way the game had become a business rather than a sport.

I have to be honest and say, having seen both the Push and Run and Double-winning sides, we were spoilt. We should have realised these halcyon days would never return, and thereafter everything seemed an anti-climax.

In later years, my late Dad and I would discuss the Glory-Glory Days and agreed how lucky we were to have been there. This was without doubt the greatest club side I ever saw and it was such a privilege to watch them playing football of the highest quality, with good sportsmanship and with an eye to entertaining while winning in style. Thanks Nick, Danny, Jimmy, Dave, Cliff and all the other players for producing a style of football that at club level I have yet to see equalled.

I like what Harry has been doing with the modern Spurs. He is old school and knows how the game can and should be played.

But take it from me, it will never be quite the same as back in the 1950s and 1960s, when Spurs – as the old jazz standard goes – were so easy to love, so easy to idolize all others above.

Yes, they were the kings of swing.

IVOR DAVIS

Occupation: Journalist/Author
Age: 73
Location: California via Clapton
Spurs fan since: 1948-49
All-time favourite player: Cliff Jones

Ivor and his wife Sally are a famous writing couple in Los Angeles. He emigrated to the USA in 1960 as a bright young journalist, and has since filled acres of newspaper and magazine space around the world, and his books include his experiences of touring with The Beatles and a remarkable focus on Charles Manson that helped bring the serial killer to justice. He was a top-flight amateur left winger with Clapton and has never shaken off the Spurs bug.

OMIGOSH! I've been gone from Hackney and White Hart Lane for – are you ready for this – 50 years. I've been living in Southern California for half a century. That's the community where the seasons are so monotonous that you go to bed when you are 21, and next morning when you wake up you're seventy! I kid you not.

So pardon my sentimental journey recounting my passion for the Beautiful Game, and the vivid boyhood memories of trekking regularly to see Spurs play. That was way back in the Fifties. (Hands up anyone in the room who remembers the Fifties?)

I was a teenager who absorbed the game voraciously. I was a useful left winger (not politically but physically), and I played three games at the weekend – Saturday morning, Sunday morning and Sunday afternoon.

But never on a Saturday afternoon when Tottenham were at home. That was reserved for supporting Spurs, and after the game we'd assemble outside our local newsagents waiting for delivery of the last classified editions of the evening papers (the *Star, News and Standard*), with all the up to date League scores. Back then we didn't have a telly. That was the privilege of the rich and maybe famous.

But back to Spurs.

As a soccer-mad kid growing up in Upper and Lower Clapton, I was an addict when it came to the Lilywhites. Although the word addict was not then part of my vocabulary.

To see the Spurs home games I went with a group of like-minded pals and took the 653 bus to Stamford Hill, and then walked all the way – three and a bit miles – to the stadium. No booking tickets ahead, or the luxury of having a season ticket.

You had to get there early to establish your right to standing space. We plonked down our ninepence for the privilege of standing behind the goal. Yes, I did say stand. Seats? They, like television, were for the rich.

Watching Spurs from the terraces behind the goal was something you didn't forget easily. By kick-off time for the big games 60,000-plus spectators would be shoehorned into the ground and bodies were packed shoulder to shoulder. If you sneezed six people fell over. It was body tight to body, and when the crowd swayed you swayed with them, sometimes with perilous results. It was a huge challenge to go to the loo or try to get a slurp of tea in a cardboard cup.

There was no way a small lad like me (I now stand a towering 5 foot four and three quarter inches but was much shorter then) could struggle to the urinal or the refreshment booth without help. And then I had to fight my way back for the second half. So they would pass my tiny frame over the crowd like a suitcase.

But who really cared? It was all part and parcel of the exciting experience. All that mattered was that on the pitch Spurs strutted their lovely stuff and we were hypnotized by the action.

Those were the days of stars athletes like Alf Ramsey (the general and a key exponent of the push and run style). And the rugged Bill Nicholson trying to deal with those pesky Froggatt boys, Sheffield Wednesday's Redfern and Jack, his cousin at Pompey. Or Tottenham trying to snuff out the danger of Portsmouth's 'Mount Rushmore' centre forward, Dougie Reid. Those were the days when Pompey were back to back League champions before Arthur Rowe's Spurs took over as the masters.

We thrilled to the lightning runs of Spurs' outside left Cliff Jones when he arrived from Swansea in 1958 for what was then a mindblowing £35,000. There was talk of the game going mad because of such a huge fee being paid. Today it would not cover half a week's wages for many in the Premier League.

By then I was doing my National Service, with a cushy London posting that meant I was able to get to the Lane for every home match. Cliff was a forerunner to fellow Welshman Gareth Bale, and for several years was considered the best – and certainly the quickest – outside-left in the world. Okay, so the Jones boy didn't jig or dribble his way to the goal line like the wizard Stanley Matthews. But he did a 100 metres straight sprint down the left wing. Eat your heart out Usain Bolt.

Back then at his peak, Cliff picked up 17 quid a week, plus the fat bonus of four pounds for a win, and two for a draw.

But I digress, with economic facts that must sound nonsense to today's generation. White Hart Lane and Spurs was the   regular escape hatch for working class lads like me.

Players were our flesh and blood movie stars, our giants. I remember Cheeky Chappie Eddie Baily, the Spurs and England forward who lived near me in Clapton. When we spotted him on the street it was akin to seeing Elvis.

On the field we marvelled at skipper Danny Blanchflower, the stylish Belfast playmaker. Danny Boy had a wit as sharp and pinpointed as his passes, as I later discovered when we were both scribbling for *Express* newspapers. It was Danny, of course, who led Spurs to the fantastic Cup and League double in l960-61, the season that I took off for my adventure across the Pond.

From behind the goal at the Lane, we admired visiting 'keepers like Charlton's Sam Bartram and Arsenal's flyng Welshman Jack Kelsey. Mind you they couldn't hold a candle to our very own Ted Ditchburn.

And those were the days when we hissed at rivals from Woolwich Nomads like the tall gangling centre-half Les and dribbling winger Denis, who was better known for his leg sweep than his left peg.

League games were the highlight of our schoolboy lives. I have fond memories of Cardiff coming to White Hart Lane. The hometown crowd booed when a group of somewhat inebriated Welsh supporters, who had made the long trek to London, rushed on to the pitch and planted leeks on the centre spot.

Growing up in Clapton, leeks were some kind of exotic veggie to a kid weaned on cabbage and the odd brussel sprout. Anyway, I wondered, 'Why the hell are they planting those giant onions on the pitch?' I had no idea that leeks were the Welsh national symbol.

My first-hand experiences and admiration for Spurs (never, never Hotspurs) did not decline when I headed to seek my fortune on the West Coast of the USA. Alas, games were not televised live to California for many decades, and so I could only avidly read about the continuing Spurs fortunes, including the antics of that human scoring machine Jimmy Greaves.

But I did watch my old Spurs hero Alf Ramsey steering England to the 1966 World Cup from the posh Beverley Hills house of musical genius Leslie Bricusse, with Dickie Attenborough and Tony Newley among our enraptured companions. By then I had survived a nationwide United States tour with The Beatles, and I covered the following four World Cup finals for CBS radio. I have reported more than 20 world title fights in Las Vegas, been the West Coast correspondent for a string of newspapers, and wrote a book about serial killer Charles Manson that was used by the prosecution to help convict him. Yet for all this I still warmly remember my days on the Tottenham terraces as if they were yesterday.

Now in the 21st century I am once again a renewed Spurs fan. Thanks to Fox Soccer in

Ex-Spurs hero Sir Alf Ramsey ... Ivor Davis saw him as the Tottenham general and then steering England to a memorable triumph in the 1966 World Cup finals

America, I can follow the adventures of Gareth, Luka, VDV and Harry Rednapp's gang. And not surprisingly I have become something of an armchair expert. Okay, so Les Medley, Sonny Walters and the old favourites have been replaced by a bunch of players with unpronounceable names. No more Smiths and Joneses, Browns, Bakers and Allens. Now you have to get your tongue around names like Adebayor, Luka Modric and Rafa Van Der Vaart, and it's good to see a young (well, young to me) Englishman like Scott Parker making his mark in the Lilywhite shirt.

But regardless of the names, the Spurs spirit is still there, and as I watch from 5,500 miles away at 7 am in my California aerie, I just know I would have easily tapped in that right wing cross from Aaron. And blind ole Riley – on the third instant replay – I knew it should never have been a penalty, or a red card.

And as I watch the screen, memories come flooding back of those days when I was a nipper on the jam-packed White Hart Lane terraces. A long time ago, a long way away. But the mantra has not changed: 'Come on you Spurs.'

RONNIE WOLMAN

Occupation: Home decor and fabric specialist
Age: 64
Location: Toronto, Canada, via London
Spurs fan since: Birth
All-time favourite player: Dave Mackay
Website: www.spurscanada.ca

Ronnie is a prolific contributor to spurscanada.ca, warming the ether with his passion for Spurs. He is excited about the return to the flowing football of the Double side.

It sounded like a good idea at the time. Alan Corper and I – he was a good friend from school, albeit a Gooner – decided we would go and see Tottenham play Crewe Alexandra in the F.A. Cup replay at the Lane. We were both 12 years old, and set out from our Camden Town school at 4.15pm and walked all the way – a little matter of six miles – to Tottenham High Road for the 7.30 start. It was a year before the amazing Double, and although we were playing some good football we had been held to a shock draw at Crewe on the Saturday. I wanted to be at the Lane to see us finish the job,

We got there early and found a couple of spots in the Shelf, underneath the East stand and very close to the Paxton Road end. The Lane was packed, and both of us being quite short it was difficult to get a clear view of the pitch. We fought to find openings here and there to watch snatches of the game.

As you probably know, we didn't just beat Crewe, we annihilated them as Spurs gave a taste of what was to be the future. It was the start of some glorious nights that the club were going to have both domestically and in Europe.

It was such a high-scoring affair it not only gave me the enjoyment of destroying the opposition, but also a chance to see some great goals. Both Alan and I had to hang on to the barrier or get on tip toes for a minute or two to see many of the 15 goals scored. We won 13-2 – a crushing win by what was to become one of the best sides in England,

The forward line that night featured two of the greatest creative players we have ever had, John White and also Tommy 'The Charmer' Harmer, a Tom Thumb of a player who was a brilliant artist whose peak fell between the Push and Run and Double sides.

White and Harmer were of two different Spurs generations, and here they were playing together on the same team on this day.

A year earlier I had watched us from the old stuffy West Stand chew up the Toffees 10-4, heralding Billy Nicholson's first game as manager. I sat with my Dad and occupied his brother's season ticket seat as we watched spellbound as Tottenham dissected Everton.

These two games were strong messages from the years before the Double that we were setting the stage for something much bigger than we had ever done before, in a style that was borne out of the past and yet inspired the future. I cannot say either one of these games actually made me fall in love with Spurs. The union of my mother and father in 1946 really set the tone. It was a kind of arranged marriage for me, supported by my Dad and endorsed by my Uncles on both sides – all of whom were Tottenham supporters.

My father loved good football and it was the 1950 team that really had an impact on him. Eddie Baily was his favourite and he always said he could turn on a sixpence.

I did see that 1950 team, but have little recollection. It was 1950 and I was two-and-a-half when my Dad carried me into the stadium to watch what was a 7-0 thrashing of Newcastle. It must have had an effect on my psyche!

My father, an amateur football analyst and self-proclaimed critic, was always very perceptive of the way we played. He often wrote letters to the papers and more often than not the newspapers printed them. His insight made me look at the game beyond the basic facts.

Uncle Moe bought me a birthday present book in the 1950s about the history of Spurs, and in 1957 I went with my Mum to Canada for a holiday and Tottenham were there on tour. I watched them play Celtic and a local team, winning both games. My Uncle Mickey in Toronto got me in to see the players at half-time, and I swapped Hellos with the one and only Danny Blanchflower! In 1960 my Dad bought me a season ticket high up in the gods where I watched the games with my uncle Moe. The view had a profound effect on the way I saw a match. What was lost in the dizzy heights of the East Stand of the intimacy of seeing our heroes close up was gained in insight of the flow of our game. If the Old stand on the other side or right behind the goal was more like the trenches, the East stand was a command centre overlooking the land and unlocking the game's strategies. It was up in the East Stand which towered above it all that we saw the ebb and flow of the game. We watched the way our moves developed and this offered a very different view of the game to anywhere else.

Here you could see and feel the fluency of our beautiful football. This was 1960-61 and we knew how to create and develop our attacks and defend against the enemy.

Danny was our captain and not just in name. He controlled the game, its tempo and inspired its movement. On the other side it was Dave Mackay, full of power but also talent, who led our team into battle and backed down to no man.

From where I sat, watching our defence, one could see clearly that there was no attempt to give the offside trap a voice in our system. We defended by defending. Man behind the ball. Man behind the man.

Blanchflower often backed off when defending pointing to his defenders where to be and where to run. He often employed a retreating defence to snare back the ball after he had drawn them into a net where everyone was fully marked. Then Danny would pick up

Eddie 'The Cheeky Chappie' Baily, who could turn on a sixpence

the ball and move up in the middle third and develop the next attack.

On the Mackay left side it was Dave and behind him Ron Henry, who was totally in awe of the dynamic Scot in front of him. Mackay, who pushed out his chest like a Highlander marching to war, gave confidence to the whole team around him but especially Henry, who became a different player when Dave was around. If there were a pair of bagpipes handy, Henry would have been the man playing them in honour of Mackay. On attack it was mostly the cerebral Irishman Blanchflower who took the ball up the field, and immediately created space. To do that you need players that understand where to run and there was none better that our very own ghost, John White, to find that space. White, instinctively comprehended Danny's game well and found space to work in and fed the speedsters Jones and Dyson on the wings, and our burly centre forward Bobby Smith. He was one of the last great old-style centre-forwards, and he was complemented by a man who was also instrumental in bringing goals at that time, Les Allen.

The three at the back were Baker, Norman and Henry, a solid group and backed by the ever safe goalkeeper Bill Brown (later I moved to Canada, where I met Bill Brown by chance, and he gave me his bird's eye view of the Double season)

They were all part of this amazing flow. We were a machine and like the Beatles and many other talented groups, were much bigger than the sum of their parts. Yes we were a team where all played their own particular instruments, their talents quite individual but it all congruently melded together into a cohesive band

It is impossible to explain what a wonderful feeling it was to watch us not only win but win with style.

Just as Push and Run was beyond the capacity of most other teams in 1950, so Billy Nicholson's 60-61 Tottenham had developed a more sophisticated version.

Billy and Danny expanded the concept with great movement, sublime passing and a knack for finding space This was the beauty of Tottenham, and it is what I fell in love with. It wasn't one particular game or one shot. Our game offered a completely different language.

That summer we signed Jimmy Greaves. He was coming to join our wonderful team. It was the equivalent of signing Messi today. My Dad showed me a Pathé News film of the 1959-60 Real Madrid against Eintracht Frankfurt European Cup Final. Parts of the film were in slow motion and like a beautifully choreographed dance. I said, "That's the way WE play!"

It wasn't one moment, game by game my love for Tottenham got stronger. We played heavenly football and in Europe. all in white too; shades of that exceptional Real team of the time.

We reached the 1962 European Cup semi-finals, and very nearly knocked out powerful Benfica. It seemed like destiny and a date with Real, with both teams in full white would have been a match made in heaven.

That is a high spot to reach. It contains all the elements. In the past we have had a few good teams, and we have had absolutely great players like Klinsmann, Ginola, Lineker, Hoddle and Berbatov. What we always needed was to have a whole bunch of players that could gel and make greatness happen.

That is why am so excited today. As I contribute this chapter to the first Spurs Writers' Club book, our team has more potential than I've seen in over 50 years . The flow is there again. The game is faster and the competition is tougher, but we are showing at times aspects of that 60s team.

The song has changed but the team is in tune again. The flow, good movement, exceptional vision is back again. The talent of Harry Redknapp's team gives us good reason to be optimistic that the boys are back and that the Cockerel up in the east stand is crowing loud again. Suddenly, it's as beautiful as a Canadian sunset.

I'm sure Bill and Danny are Up There beaming, and their spirits are alive providing the light to brighten our immediate future. We are flowing again.

KEVIN FIELD

Occupation: Retired civil servant
Age: 61
Location: Lincoln via London
Spurs fan since: 1958
All-time favourite player: Alan Gilzean

Kevin is a retired civil servant, who follows the fortunes of Tottenham from his home in Lincoln, where he lives with his wife of thirty-six years, Janet, who is also an avid Spurs fan. They have two grown children and two grandchildren.

THIS is the story of my journey lasting nine years, before I was allowed and able to see Spurs play a game in the flesh. It is the story of heartbreak, frustration, obedience and annoyance, but nevertheless a story that – looking back – took place in a totally different world in which parents had to be obeyed and rules observed.

My love affair with Spurs began in the autumn of 1958 when, at the tender age of eight, I accompanied my Mum and Dad from our home in Luton on a shopping trip to Tottenham. Why we would go to Tottenham was a complete mystery, and unfortunately remains so as both my parents have passed on. I doubt that Tottenham High Road was the Brent Cross Shopping Centre of the 1950s. Perhaps I found the answer while researching my family history and discovering that my dad had numerous family members born, bred and living in the Tottenham and Edmonton district.

I would like to be able to say that the affair began on October 11 1958, which of course was Billy Nicholson's first match in charge when we beat Everton 10-4. What a story that would be, but alas I still have no idea of the exact date. I do, however, remember very clearly that we were in the High Road when I heard this almighty roar. Having never been near to a football ground never mind seeing a match, I had no idea what the noise was. I asked my Dad and was told that Tottenham were playing at home and the ground was just up the road. But I have the dream that the noise was maybe – just maybe – one of the ten goals against Everton hitting the back of the net, but a dream it must remain.

The following day I looked at the football results in the Sunday paper and was puzzled that after Tottenham there was a letter H. Other clubs had names such as City, Rovers, Town or Athletic. Dad told me the H stood for Hotspur. That was enough for me. I was hooked by such a fabulous out of the ordinary name and became at that moment, an unofficial Spurs Football Supporter.

Before I could persuade Dad to take me to a game, we moved up north to a village about fifteen miles from Liverpool. The local children thought me unusual as I spoke in a funny accent and supported a team with a strange name. The other children in the main supported Everton or Liverpool, who were at that time in the Second Division. Ian St John, a star player for the Reds, lived close by and could often be seen washing his own car! No high walls and gates to hide behind. He like all footballers was an ordinary man just doing ordinary things. Players were so different then.

I started my persuasive tactics again in an attempt to see my beloved team, who by then were beating most sides and scoring hatfuls of goals. Dad said that he would only take me to Everton as the two Manchester clubs were too far away. In reality he did not really want to take me as he was not a bona fide Spurs supporter. His team was whichever London side won, starting with West Ham and working from there in no particular order.

The following season was the one that everyone remembers 60/61. Spurs began like a steam train, winning the first eleven games. Even the other boys in the village school began to take an interest in my team. Suddenly I was not the supporter of a team with a strange name. I supported the team that the whole country was talking about.

I pestered my dad again to take me to Everton. His excuse this time was that it was too close to Christmas. Looking now at the attendance, 61,052 didn't agree with him and went to see their heroes lose 3-1 to the Team of The Century, as Spurs were being called. My only success was seeing the Cup Final live on a small black and white TV with a nine-inch screen. I was ecstatic when we beat Leicester 2-0 to win the Double. I thought that maybe the next season dad would relent and take me to see my first match.

Before the 61/62 season began, we moved yet again, this time to Staffordshire, a county that had no local teams playing in the First Division. I had to be content reading the papers and watching what little football there was on the TV. This went on for eighteen months before we moved to Hertfordshire. By this time I was aged twelve and even though we lived thirty minutes by train from Kings Cross and then the direct 73 bus service, my parents thought me too young to go to White Hart Lane on my own. It would take a further five years – the wilderness years – of pestering and arguing before I would go to see my beloved Spurs in the flesh.

During this period my favourite player at that time, John White, was tragically killed by lightning while playing a solo round of golf in the summer of 1964. I was heartbroken. I had to have a new favourite, but who would it be? Later that year a player with a strange name joined the club with the so-called strange name, supported by a boy with a so-called strange accent. It was a match made in heaven – and my hero worship with Alan Gilzean began.

The great Spurs team from the double season had been slowly replaced by another one of

Portrait of John White, the much-mourned Ghost of White Hart Lane

fresh-faced players bought from all corners of Britain. It took some time for them to knit together, but they peaked during the 66/67 season when after remaining undefeated from January, they beat Chelsea 2-1 in the first all London Cup Final. I still had not been to White Hart Lane and did not even see the match on the TV. Dad in his own inimitable way decided during the previous year that there was nothing on the 'Box' worth watching, and he sent the set back. In those days most people rented their TV sets due to their unreliability and high cost of repair.

I suppose that I must be one of the few Spurs fans to have achieved a unique double, by not seeing the 1966 World Cup Final or the 1967 FA Cup Final. It was beginning to get to me. For goodness sake I was seventeen and I remember issuing what could be counted as an ultimatum to my parents: If I was old enough to go to London with my friend (unknown to them to basically smoke and mess about), I was old enough to go to see Spurs play. In those days if a parent said no it meant no and there was no back chat and I couldn't go against their decisions. I finally got my wish to see a live Spurs game during the 67/68 season when I was seventeen and a half!

On December 2 1967, a date forever engraved on my heart, I travelled to White Hart Lane with my Dad to see Spurs play Newcastle United. It was not the dream match to start with but any match would do, I just needed to see Spurs play. I was very excited as we travelled to the game but at the same time annoyed, that my consummate moment had taken nine years to fulfil. The ticket for an unreserved seat cost nine shillings (45p) and the programme sixpence (2.5p). Yes it was another world then, and the programme usually listed the correct teams and news for each club.

We took our seats in the Paxton Road end and awaited the kick off. The teams came out to a rather subdued roar as the ground was not full. The official attendance was only 34,494 compared to crowds of 60,000 for the big games. Despite this I was so happy, with a grin from ear to ear, proudly wearing my Spurs rosette.

I looked at the players, searching in particular for my hero Alan Gilzean. Where was he, who is that in the number five shirt, certainly not Mike England whose birthday it was. Roger Hoy, never heard of him! And who's that wearing the number ten? Dennis Bond, nowhere near as good as Terry Venables! That's two big name players missing. I began to worry, where was my hero? Thank goodness there he was, easily spotted wearing the number nine, six foot tall and receding hairline. It is now forty four years on and I cannot remember a lot about the match apart from Gilzean scoring at the Paxton Road End, right in front of my eyes to earn Spurs a 1-1 draw. The crowd went wild and the noise of the feet stamping on the wooden floor of the stand was something that I had never heard before.

It didn't matter if we had won or lost, after nine years I had finally seen my beloved Spurs play. More importantly, my hero had scored the only Spurs goal. I was finally off and running and could now be classed as an official Tottenham Hotspur Football Supporter.

LOGAN HOLMES

Occupation: Retired Head Teacher
Age: 59
Location: Carrickfergus, Northern Ireland
Spurs fan since: 1964-65
All-time favourite player: Jimmy Greaves/Pat Jennings

Logan managed to include references to Spurs in school assemblies. He has always had an interest in Tottenham's glorious history and has written for Topspurs and in the CADD fanzine, as their Northern Ireland correspondent.

IT was the first Saturday in May and the prospect of an afternoon spent shopping in Belfast was hardly appealing for a nine year old boy. That visit, however, to a furniture store was to make a lasting impression which has stayed with me over almost fifty years.

Growing up in Northern Ireland in the early 1960s in a family with no sporting connections, I had no interest or knowledge of football, but that Saturday as my parents considered their options for buying a dining room suite I watched a match on a small, black and white television with a couple of sales assistants. It was the 1962 F.A. Cup Final between Burnley and Tottenham Hotspur, at the time, arguably the two best teams in the country. With three Northern Ireland internationals playing, Alex Elder and Jimmy McIlroy for Burnley and Spurs' Danny Blanchflower, there was an obvious interest for my fellow viewers. Of those three, there was one, in particular, who drew most comment – Blanchflower, the inspirational captain of Tottenham Hotspur.

Jimmy Greaves put Spurs ahead in the opening minutes, but Burnley equalised at the start of the second half. Within seconds Spurs regained the lead when Bobby Smith scored. Late in the game, it was that man, Blanchflower, who stepped up to take a penalty which would almost certainly guarantee Spurs another trophy. As the Burnley goalkeeper dived to his left, Blanchflower, the coolest person in Wembley Stadium, placed the ball in the opposite corner. Tottenham's two goal advantage had been restored and they went on to retain the F.A. Cup. I honestly don't know if my memory of Blanchflower comes from watching the game or from photographs that I have seen in subsequent years but which ever it is, the recollection of that F.A. Cup win has remained with me since May 5 1962.

In those days there was not the widespread coverage of football that we enjoy today, *Match of the Day* was still still some years away and the F.A. Cup Final was the only football shown on television – a treat, once a year. As I watched, I had no knowledge of the glorious season that Spurs had enjoyed a year earlier when they had become the first team in the 20th century to win the League and Cup 'Double'. I was oblivious to the fact that a few weeks previously they had so nearly reached the final of the European Cup. I was unaware that Jimmy Greaves had cost £99,999 because the manager hadn't wanted him to be labelled the first £100,000 player, and I didn't know that he had scored a hat-trick on his Tottenham debut or that he had predicted that he would score in the opening minutes of the Final and had duly delivered after three. Such Tottenham trivia would only become part of my life in years to come as I became more caught up in being a Spurs supporter.

Tottenham won the Cup, the dining room suite was purchased and I went home with no more interest in football than I'd had when I'd wakened that morning. Unbeknown to me, however, a tiny 'seed' of Tottenham Hotspur had been sown deep in the dark recesses of my mind, but it would be like a very slow growing plant which would need nourishment and take some considerable time to develop.

The 'seed' lay dormant for over two years and so I was to miss out on the European campaign which culminated in that wonderful evening in Rotterdam in May, 1963 when Spurs became the first British club to win a European trophy as they demolished Atletico Madrid by five goals to one in the final of the European Cup Winners' Cup.

In the summer of 1964, the Tottenham 'seed' received a little nurturing. While on holiday in the south of England, for some unaccountable reason, I tore a photograph of the Spurs squad from my uncle's copy of the *Daily Express* and took it home with me. The article which accompanied the picture detailed how Spurs' fortunes had changed in the previous couple of years. Harry Langton wrote, *'The club was on top of the world two years ago as F.A. Cup winners for the second successive year and European Cup semi-finalists. They were still top fourteen months ago when they won the European Cup Winners' Cup. Since then there have been few joys for Spurs.'* He went on to detail the injuries to Terry Medwin and Dave Mackay, the retirement of Danny Blanchflower, the departure of Bobby Smith and the tragic loss of the late John White, but despite those set-backs, he reported that Spurs were looking forward to the new season with optimism.

My collection of Tottenham memorabilia had started but that was it – a photograph. The following December when the BBC news showed the goals from the Christmas fixtures it was Tottenham's win over Nottingham Forest at White Hart Lane which stirred my interest a little more. The goals from Jimmy Robertson, Jimmy Greaves, Alan Gilzean and Terry Dyson, a mixture of 'old' and 'new' Spurs, meant they had completed the 'double' over Forest, having won at the City Ground on Boxing Day. What an unusual season it was to be, only that one success on their travels but undefeated at home – the only time in their history that Spurs have achieved that feat.

The 'seed' was developing and gaining a hold on me. On my return to school after the holidays, a friend told me of his football programme collection and how he acquired them by sending a stamped self-addressed envelope to the Secretary at each club. That was it, I was hooked and developed a regular correspondence with the Tottenham Club Secretary - my

Danny Blanchflower, Tottenham's 'Captain Marvel'

new pen-friend. My association and support of Tottenham was secure. Every fortnight a Spurs programme arrived – not like the £3.50, hundred page, colour volume we buy today but a thin, twelve page edition with no adverts which cost a mere 3d (1.5p). From this I gleaned as much information as possible about the players, matches and the club's history.

A visit to the paper shop at seven o'clock each Saturday evening became an essential part of supporting Spurs. There I would buy a copy of Ireland's *Saturday Night*, a sports paper which covered Irish League football and other sports of local interest as well as providing brief match reports for football in England. It was the Northern Ireland equivalent of the pink 'un or green 'un which appeared outside grounds around England almost immediately after the final whistle had been blown. There would be queues of fans waiting for the van to arrive with the papers so that they could check the results and reports. Such was the rush to get the papers to the grounds that if there was late drama, a last minute goal couldn't be reported. While the football papers in many English cities disappeared years ago due to developments in the media and the internet, the Northern Ireland version only ceased publication three years ago after being in existence for well over a century.

At that time, going to see Spurs at White Hart Lane was not an option, it was a pipe dream, as no-one would have thought of travelling to England to attend a match and it would be decades before budget airlines made regular trips to Tottenham a reality for me.

There is no explanation as to why I started to support Spurs. There were no family connections with the club, I don't actually think I knew where Tottenham was when I first became aware of Spurs and if it hadn't been for that shopping trip in May,1962 it might never have happened. The dining room suite which was bought that day served my parents well throughout their days and it looks as if the highs and lows of supporting Tottenham Hotspur will continue to be part of my life for some time to come.

SAM FISHER

Occupation: Production Assistant
Age: 59
Location: Brize Norton, West Oxfordshire
Spurs fan since: 1961
All-time favourite player: Cliff Jones
Blogs:
Spurs Reflections (www.spursreflections.blogspot.com)
(www.hotspursamsmusings.blogspot.com)

Sam has followed Spurs since the Double Year '61 Cup Final and was a season ticket holder in the '70s. Thirty years world-wide service in the RAF. Known as HotspurSam on the internet/Twitter

HERE we are in 2012, and I am 59 years young, so it is no mystery of arithmetical calculation to realise that I was nothing more than a rosy cheeked urchin in short-trousers and wide braces way back in the distant days of the early1960s, just when such a cheeky chappie was of an age to discover 'football'. To be precise, my Glory Glory moment took place over the weekend of May 6 and 7 1961. Guessed what it is yet? If not, it is doubtful you have yet had a Lilywhite blood transfusion.

It was, of course, the weekend of the 1961 Cup Final, when Spurs completed the historic 'Double'. Before then I didn't know what a cup final was let alone a double, and yet the occasion left me wide-eyed, wondrous, enthralled, and a Spurs fan for life.

The exploits of my new heroes, and the magic dust they sprinkled over me, left such an impression that my life has never been the same again – I thank them and I damn them (nicely) at the same time.

In the following half century I have had many occasions to continue to marvel at the exploits of the men in Lilywhite, and many a time I have been given just cause to cuss them, but I have never regretted my lot at being a Spurs supporter. To have been selected to be a chosen one, is both an honour and a privilege, which is only bestowed on we the blessed. The good has outweighed the bad, and the bad has made the good taste all the sweeter.

To be able to understand why that weekend and that particular event could be so magical to this young boy we need to understand the times and to bring them into perspective, with the help of a little social anthropological history.

I was eight years old, and lived in the little sea-side town of Bangor, in the county of

Down, Northern Ireland Apart from a kick around in the school playground with jumpers for goal posts I knew next to nothing about football. Back then, Cowboys and Indians took all my interest and Roy Rogers, in his white Stetson and riding his dazzling white horse Trigger, were my heroes, enjoyed from the stalls on my Saturday morning visits to the local cinema.

One of the reasons I knew so little of football is that I was brought up by my single-parent mother and big sister (eight years older), so there was no man or father figure in my life, nor any talk or activity of manly pursuits. Back in the 1960s life was so much different than today. There was no Child Allowance or other benefits. Whatever money my mother had to keep herself and me and my sister, she had to earn. Lack of child-care facilities meant that my mum could only be a Mrs Mop to fit in her working life with her responsibility as a parent.

I was a 'Latch Key Kid'. Additionally, I was the product of a short-lived mixed marriage, and that in Northern Irish terms means a marriage from both sides of the sectarian divide, and so forms of ostracisation were another obstacle for my poor Mum to overcome. In other words, she didn't have money or time to waste on such frivolities as newspapers, magazines or comics, and so I knew very little outside of my own little world, and yet I was happy enough in my ignorance, and of course that ignorance included sport in general and football in particular.

My friend Raymond and I played safely in 'our' street, hide and seek, kick ball, Cowboys and Indians, hop-scotch and the like. There weren't many cars about in those days, and so we had plenty of free space in which to play.

Televisions were also an item of luxury and beyond my Mum's purse. We had an old valve radio which took five minutes to warm up. I suspect the football results were read out each week, but I wouldn't have taken any notice of boring men reading out lots of boring details that went on forever. I would have tuned into a repeat of Dick Barton Special Agent, or would have been anxiously waiting to listen to Jimmy Clitheroe, the great Jimmy Edwards or even Kenneth Horne or the Navy Lark.

However, there were a handful of tellys in the street, and rushing home from school or at weekends we would be invited around to some one's house to watch The Lone Ranger, Ivanhoe, Bronco Lane, Just William, and, of course, the white-hatted hero on his white horse, Roy Rogers.

Then it happened. One Saturday in May 1961 whilst out playing, I saw my Uncle John's car pull up outside our house. This was good news as I usually got two-bob (10p) pressed into my hand at the end of the visit – that became my pocket money for the next four weeks. This time he visited with my Aunt Anne and two girl cousins, who would usually tease and nip me on the arm and legs (but it was worth it for the two-bob).

This particular visit was with a special purpose. They were upgrading their TV from 425 lines to the new-fangled, super-duper set with 625 lines that could receive ITV as well as the BBC. So we were being given their old black and white set.

It took ages to set up – 'Hurry up Uncle John, hurry up!' It was the indoor aerial that took the time and I was getting agitated, and really desperate to sit down and watch Roy Rogers chasing down the baddies on MY telly.

At last it was all ready for blast off, but what a disappointment! Once the grainy lines settled down I was most disappointed to see a boring looking old (to me) man chatting away, and worse still, he wasn't Roy Rogers, or an American film star, but he sounded just like me with a Northern Irish accent, and he had a stupid name – Blanchflower!

Unbeknown to me it was a thing called Cup Final Day and this Blanchflower chap was to play in a football match for a team called Tottenham Hotspur against a team called Leicester City. Now this was promising as I had never seen men play football before.

I couldn't quite get my tongue around the exotic and exciting name of Tottenham Hotspur (think of Ossie Ardiles with an Ulster accent – and you've got it). It was the pre-match interview stage that I was watching, with the players getting on the coach to go to some place called Wembley. I was tending to side with the Tottenham team as this Blanchflower man was the only one from Northern Ireland and so I wanted him to win.

The match eventually started. The females chatted away, and Uncle John and I settled down to watch the match. By now I was enthralled at the sight and sound of the crowd, the vast number of people. There were more people there surely than lived in the whole of Bangor, maybe even in the whole of Belfast – this was wonderful. Everyone was happy and cheering and waving rattles and flags – and the marching band.

"Uncle John does this happen every week?" – "No".

"Uncle John does Bangor have a team?" – "Yes". WOW!

I followed the game in black and white, not knowing who was who, but as with my games of Cowboys and Indians I wanted the team in white to be the good guys, just like the white-hatted Roy Rogers. I wanted 'Totteingham' to be the good guys. So I was drawn to the team in white, but I wasn't too sure of that chicken badge on their shirts .

"Uncle John, why do they have a chicken for a badge?"

"They don't, it's a fighting cock." – WOW!

Fighting cocks fight to the end, and they never give up – right? If only the team in white was the team this Mr Blanchflower played for.

"Uncle John, which team do you want to win?" – "The team in white." – WOW! "Uncle John, which team is Mr Blanchflower playing for?" – "The team in white, Tottenham." – WOW!

"Uncle John, can I cheer for Totteringham?" – "Yes." – WOW!

By now the right-back, Chalmers, of Leicester in the black 'baddie' shirt, had been injured and the white-shirted 'goodie' team was playing better, and they eventually scored two goals and won the game. Yes *my* team had won the match.

Then came the presentation, and lots of people where slapping the players on the back and

Danny Blanchflower is chaired by "the goodies" after completing the Double

cheering and yelling, as the players went up through the crowd to receive their trophy.

They had this big thing called a Cup and they ran around the pitch holding it aloft and showing it off to the cheering crowd, and this Blanchflower was their leader, and he was very good – and he talked just like me – WOW!

I dashed out to see Raymond to tell him about my telly and the football, and we played kick-ball for hours and hours until it got dark. I was Blanchflower, I was Smith, I was Dyson, I was Mackay, I was Cliff Jones. I was everyone, and even Brown scored. I went to bed that night very excited at all the wonders I had seen and Uncle John pressed a half crown into my palm as he ruffled my hair. The last image I had from my telly that night was from the News, which showed the Tottenham players, dressed up to the nines, going into a hotel to celebrate their win. I had a glass of milk and a chocolate biscuit. Apparently I had it wrong, because they hadn't won a Cup after all, but something called a double – I was confused.

Now any one of those glorious things would have been enough to persuade a young rascal to be excited by these heroes in white, but which particular one was the Damascene moment when my blood turned to white and blue from the common-or-garden ordinary r*d?

The next day whilst watching my new telly and the news came on once again, and all of a sudden there were my heroes riding on top of an open top bus, holding two trophies – (aha, the Double), whilst the whole world, as it seemed to me, came out to cheer them on. I didn't know things like this happened. Where did all these people come from? Where was Tottenham anyhow?

Because the throng of people was so great it seemed to take forever for the bus to travel to the Town Hall, where the players came out to yet more rapturous cheers, and showed off their trophies. Apparently what they had done hadn't been done before that century – WOW!

That was it, I'm sure of it. It wasn't Mr Blanchflower, or the singing cheering crowd, or the marching band, nor Mackay's tackles, Blanchflower's passes, Dyson's runs, or the goals nor the post-match celebrations, maybe the white shirts and badge helped, but in reality it was the open top bus parade on May 7 1961 – that was the moment my heart belonged to Tottenham Hotspur, my Glory Glory moment.

All I can say is a big thank you to my Uncle John, and of course to Roy Rogers for wearing his white hat – otherwise things would probably have turned out completely different for me, and only for the worse. If I had liked the baddies, good grief – I might have become a Leicester City supporter!

I love my Spurs, and it is Good to be a Spur, and God Bless The Double Team of '61.

DAVID GUTHRIE
Occupation: Consultant
Age: 58
Location: Wokingham, Berkshire
Spurs fan since: 1960
All-time favourite player: Dave Mackay

David is a contracts management consultant in the Oil and Gas Industry and has worked all over the world during the past 35 years. A keen collector of Spurs memorabilia, his prize possession is a collection of every single home and away programme from the historic 1960/61 Double season.

I CAN'T really remember a time that I actually had no knowledge of some sort of the Spurs. It was my Mum who was the football fan in the house. My parents hailed from Ireland and had no particular footballing allegiances when they set up house in Wood Green in 1948. My Mum, however, always loved the underdog and, at the time, Tottenham were still in the old Second Division, while Arsenal had just won the League Championship: So she became a 'Spur' and I guess that is where it started.

My Dad had no interest in the game at the time – he had his own 'Damascus' experience when he took me to White Hart Lane in 1965 and that becomes a whole new story for another day.

I only have vague memories of the famous 1960-61 season. Things became a lot clearer for me the following season, and in particular the disappointment of losing to Benfica in the semi-final of the European Cup, and then the 1962 Cup Final victory over Burnley at Wembley. My Mum also finally got the message over to me in the summer of that year that winning the 'Double' did not mean two successive FA Cup Final victories. So the concept of the Football League Championship as a competition also landed upon me at the same time.

In October 1962, I was finally taken to White Hart Lane for the first time with a school friend of mine, Clive, and his Dad. It was Arsenal and a 4-4 draw. It was the colour of the occasion (black and white TV days) and smell (orange peel and cigarettes) that I recall most vividly from that match. And also the sight of Dave Mackay, who scored the first ever goal I saw at White Hart Lane. Another match and another draw – this time with Everton – followed in early December. This time I was only enthused by the fact that the match appeared to finish at night time!

Santa brought me my first Spurs kit at Christmas (still my personal favourite to this day) and we then experienced the worst winter for many years, and there was very little football played until almost March 1963.

Spurs had also by this stage progressed to the quarter-final of the European Cup Winners' Cup and were drawn to play FC Slovan of Bratislava, with the first leg being played on a mud heap in Czechoslovakia on Tuesday, March 6. The Czech national team had reached the 1962 World Cup Final in Chile and their squad contained several of the Slovan Team.

In particular there was the goalkeeper, Viliam Schroif, who was known as the 'Rubber Man', presumably in reference to his athletic ability. Just like the man acknowledged at that time as the World's No.1 Goalkeeper, Lev Yashin, Schroif sported an all-black kit. Slovan were therefore no pushover and more than demonstrated this in the first leg, albeit for a relatively poor return of just a 2-0 victory. Bill Brown, who is often overlooked in the Ditchburn/Jennings debate but still a very accomplished goalkeeper nonetheless, had the game of his life and almost single-handedly stopped it from being four, five or even six-nil to Slovan.

And so the following Saturday we were at 'the Lane' for a home match with WBA. Back again the following morning to join a huge queue that seemed to stretch over to Northumberland Park to purchase our tickets for the second-leg on the Thursday, March 15 (Yes, a Thursday, which became familiar as a European footballing day in 2011-12). Unbeknown to me at the time, I was now set to experience my first taste of one of the fabled 'Glory Glory' European Nights at White Hart Lane.

Unlike my three previous matches, this time something was very different. I was strangely nervous – to the point I couldn't eat my dinner before we left for the match. I realised that I was worried that I could see Spurs end up being beaten and dumped out of the Cup. Little did I know that this was my first taste of a series of pre-match nerves that nearly 50 years later have never abated – in fact if anything they are now becoming worse with the passage of time.

My Mum decided to come as well and the four of us got ready to leave. On the way out of the door Clive's Dad warned both of us not to start crying if Spurs lost as there was, he explained, a very good chance that this could happen. Oh God – I really was nervous now!

We arrived at White Hart Lane and were squashed in amongst a mass of bodies – the crowd was over 60,000. It was also my first mid-week match and we were later in arriving than if it had been a Saturday. As such, it meant that we couldn't get to our usual position at the front of the Lower East stand and near the corner flag of the Paxton Road End. We

Bill Brown, Greavsie, Danny Blanchflower, Dave Mackay, John White and Cliff Jones on FA Cup parade after beating Burnley 3-1 at Wembley in 1962

were actually near the halfway line, although still on the Paxton side, and what seemed to be only a little way down on the terrace.

As usual, Clive and I had our little wooden benches to stand on in order to see the match – but to no avail. I could only see as far as the edge of the penalty area at the Park Lane End. We were absolutely jam-packed. The noise and crowd were terrifying to a 10-year old – yet somehow totally enthralling. I was hanging on to my Mum for dear life.

What's that down the front – some funny men dressed in robes with wigs walking round with placards proclaiming that belief in God will grant Spurs victory (or something to that effect). Clive told me that these were the famous 'Tottenham Angels' that only appeared for European matches.

The players were now out on the field – and this first time of seeing Spurs in their all-white European strip left its mark on me.

The noise now ramped up to deafening as the game got under way. Completely different to modern day – apart from the collective rendering of 'Glory, Glory Hallelujah' – it was just an ear-splitting roar each time Tottenham went on the attack.

It seemed like forever to the first goal (actually 31 minutes) and prior to that, at the end

I could see, Slovan hit the post and my heart almost went into my stomach.

I managed to see a ball come out to my hero, Mackay, and I saw the swing of the powerful left leg and that's all I was able to see. The unbelievable explosion of noise that followed told me that we were at last on the scoresheet and perhaps could now get back into the game.

However, this was the Tottenham Hotspur of the Double-era; the Tottenham Hotspur that could – and often did - overpower and crush another team in a matter of minutes. And so it was the case in this match. Two more goals by Jimmy Greaves and Bobby Smith, neither of which I could see, quickly followed in that last 15 minutes before half-time. The noise now reached thunderous levels – and my little voice was attempting to add to the euphoria! Never mind – I was now smitten with the atmosphere.

So, we now went into the second-half ahead 3-2 on aggregate. More importantly to me at the time, I could now see clearly the end to which the Spurs were attacking. Three more goals followed in that half, and Spurs ran out 6-0 winners on the night and 6-2 on aggregate. Clive and I were joking towards the end that we now knew why Schroif was known as the 'Rubber Man' – it was because he was very good at bending over to pick the ball out of all corners of the net!

Almost fifty years later, I can still see the Slovan players very clearly in their all-blue kit and I can still hear that deafening roar when the all-white knights called the Spurs went on the charge; but most of all I can still see the sixth and final goal scored by John White, the 'Ghost of White Hart Lane'. He came from nowhere to intercept a cross-field pass and moved forward like a gazelle across the muddy pitch, ball at feet and totally under control. As the Rubber Man came out to narrow the angle, the Ghost just simply – and in one movement – placed the ball along the ground into the far corner of the netting. Simple – and game over!

In 1984 the Club produced a video of the 'Glory Glory Nights' including a Pathé News film of the match – and I finally did see those first three goals. Well, actually the second and third. In true Pathé style of the time, the only thing they captured of Mackay's goal was Schroif picking the ball out of the net!

The game was very well summed up in the opening paragraph of the match report by Laurie Pignon of the now defunct *Daily Sketch*:

> *Spurs did more than slam Slovan for six. They were reborn in all the emotional screaming and singing glory of the massacre at White Hart Lane last night.*

However, for me it was the night that I experienced the tension, the excitement and finally the jubilation and euphoria that comes with being a committed football fan in a moment of final victory.

That was the night that I was born as a Spurs Supporter – for life.

DAVID BROOKS

Occupation: Retired civil servant, currently running his own Waste Cosultancy
Age: 57
Location: Ampthill, Bedfordshire, via Darlington
Spurs fan since: 1961
All-time favourite player: Jimmy Greaves

David, married to Caron, spent 35 years in the Civil Service before early retirement four years ago. Now runs his own waste consultancy, advising local authorities. Enjoys walking his two black labradors; playing golf and photography. On the Spurs season ticket waiting list.

AGED seven years old and sitting on my Granddad's knee watching the 1961 FA Cup Final, I thought I was witnessing England in action. On a black and white television, Spurs appeared just like the team I had watched previously on the box. Club football was not televised in those days and England always played in white shirts. I was told that the team in white shirts were "dirty Spurs" by my Geordie Granddad. The fact that Spurs were not playing Newcastle United probably meant that I had free rein to support whomever I pleased on this occasion. They were playing Leicester City – and they didn't sound as good as "Spurs" or indeed, the more noble sounding "Tottenham Hotspur". Moreover, I used to buy the Hotspur comic every week!

If that had been Newcastle playing against either Leicester or Spurs that day I would have led an altogether different football life.

My family were all avid Newcastle fans. And I am from Darlington. The Quakers were in the Fouth Division. Everyone's team was either Newcastle or Sunderland. Manchester United were everyone's "second" team following the tragic Munich air crash in 1958, so I had my work cut out to maintain my choice.

I cannot remember, however, anyone ever trying to "persuade" me to change my new found allegiance. Perhaps that's because the Magpies were relegated in 1961 and didn't get promoted again until the 1964- 65 season.

In any case, can you imagine trying to convince me that Spurs were not worth following and that Newcastle were the correct team to support? Spurs win the Double and Newcastle are relegated. No brainer – even at seven!

I suppose I chose the successful team of the day and rejected the failures.

I have a theory that you are given a team when you are in primary school and it stays with you all of your days. That's how it happened for me. And so I had to wait a long time to get to see Spurs live for the first time. Four and a half years! They appeared lots of times on TV playing in the European Cup – Dukla Prague and Benfica spring to mind. And of course the European Cup Winners' Cup.

I particularly remember the 1961-62 FA Cup Final against Burnley, when I watched for the first time the greatest goal scorer of all time, Jimmy Greaves. I only had a couple of minutes to wait. Jimmy held up a pass, ran, jinked and then seemingly tapped a goal from the edge of the box with four or five around him!

Newcastle were eventually promoted and Spurs came to Toon on October 23 1965. My Uncle Tom (a regular at St James' Park) and my non-football supporter Dad agreed to take me and we ended up in the Leazes End with me as a small eleven year old towards the front. I was near the corner flag on the left of goal looking towards the passionate and intimidating Gallowgate End.

I was to keep my mouth shut!

I remember a sunny day, huge excitement and the smell of tobacco and beer.

Jimmy Greaves was playing! And Alan Gilzean - we'd sadly lost John White the previous year and Gilzean was one of those brought in. I was disappointed not to have seen John White play, he was another hero. Kids are selfish sometimes.

Greavsie came across to take a corner. A corner for God's sake. The fox in the box taking corners?

He looked every bit the hero. My hero! I couldn't take my eyes off him!

"Ya stink, Greaves!" a little voice from a kid no bigger than me shouted.

"No he doesn't – he's great!"

I surprised even myself with the outburst and felt the immediate disdain of those around me, including my Uncle Tom.

And then, Jimmy Greaves said to me...

"Thanks, son."

Gawp.

I am sure he did! We were only three or four yards apart. I am positive that he did! My Dad and Uncle didn't hear it. I tried telling them afterwards that he had spoken to me.

Laughter.

Jimmy Greaves skipping past a Frank McLintock challenge

For the life of me, I cannot remember anything else about that game of football. It finished goalless and I was slightly disappointed with the result but elated with the experience.

Nobody believed me at school and I gave up trying to convince people. It is only lately, when I recount the story, that I get nods of approval.

That was the defining moment for me. No other team could or would ever supplant my obsession with Tottenham. I was a fan before that game – as much as you can be, living in the North-East – but Spurs were now the focus of my footballing future.

Years later, I met Jimmy at one of these signing events in Milton Keynes. It was the day the press announced the sale of Thierry Henry from Arsenal. We had a conversation about what good news that was for Tottenham. I didn't mention the "Thanks, son" to him and wondered why afterwards.

You know what it's like with heroes. Even at 50+ you go quiet!

There were 46,430 present in 1965. Strangely, when we played Newcastle United in 2011 at St. James' Park there were only 10 people fewer in the crowd – 46,420.

Now that is an amazing statistic, considering the amount of money that has been spent on that stadium; they haven't squeezed any more folk into the ground for a game that determined a top four place.

We should have won that game, too. Caught out in the last few minutes and Newcastle squeezed a draw.

At the time of writing, we are third. We are playing the best football in the Premier League and I am excited that we could be on the cusp of something great. Could this be our best season in 50 years?

Let's hope so! It would be nice to say to somebody like Gareth Bale, "Thanks, son ...!"

ALAN FISHER

Occupation: Director of Care for a children's charity
Age: 56
Location: Kent
Spurs fan since: Mid-60s
All-time favourite player: Jimmy Greaves
Website: www.tottenhamonmymind.com

Alan says: "I've been a season ticket holder on the Shelf, where I stood boy and man since the late 60s – through the glory years, lean times and, worst of all, the mediocre. Five minutes before kick-off I look around and there's nowhere in the world I'd rather be." His *Tottenham On My Mind* is one of the wittiest and wisest Spurs blogs on the interweb

MAY 1967, Spurs beat Sheffield United 2-0 but I don't know why I was there. What I mean is, I'm not sure why I was at White Hart Lane as opposed to any other London football ground.

Other authors in this volume will tug at your heartstrings with tales of family tradition or maybe a random trick of fate sealed their destiny. Me, I have no idea. Just always have been, as if born with it. Brown hair, brown eyes, prone to a bit of fat, Spurs fan.

Football has always fascinated me but I don't know where it comes from as my parents weren't the slightest bit interested. In the family my uncle was the one who did football. Offered terms by Leyton Orient, in the days of the maximum wage he couldn't afford to follow his dreams and turned them down. When I was 9 he took me to my first ever match. At Highbury. Having no idea of the rivalry, I cheered Arsenal to victory, 3-1 against Burnley, but on the way home nothing had changed. I knew I was a Spurs fan.

Earlier in the 2011-12 season there's a Sunderland fan on the train. He's come a long way on a cold Sunday with low expectations. Spurs have more points, better players and better prospects but he has his devotion to his club, a precious commodity for any fan these days, which he expresses in the time-honoured fashion: 'Where were you when you were s**t?'

Some 44 years on from my first match, I'm being accused of being a gloryhunter. The price of success, I suppose, although this wasn't the time to discuss how I endured the heartache and despair in between. There's no worse insult in the football vocabulary but in my formative, impressionable years the Double team were creating a legend that will last beyond my lifetime, and I recall watching the Cup Winners' Cup in '63 on television.

Ask me where I come from, the answer was 'London', and still is. Brentford and QPR were my local teams but I had no sense of West London as a place. Spurs were in London, so was I, so it was legitimate to support them. I've paid my dues.

My Dad took me to Spurs that day. Thinking about it after all these years, I suddenly realise the sacrifices my parents made to make sure their only son could watch a, to them, meaningless football match. Dad had this tiny open-all-hours sweet shop. He must have worked from 7am until 1, then mum took over while he schlepped his over-excited little boy across town.

Apart from the result I confess that I don't recollect the slightest thing about the game itself. Being there is a different matter. Close my eyes and every moment of the experience is preserved fresh and vibrant. Manor House was the nearest tube in those days, then follow the crowd to the end of the queue for the football special buses, a fleet of Routemasters direct to the ground. A rosette chosen with care regardless of the vendor's impatience, but this symbol of loyalty had to be right. A plastic cockerel on a ball, a classic that I recognised as the club's tradition. My tradition. No Olympic gold medal winner has ever been prouder than I was when Dad pinned it on my chest.

Propelled by anticipation, I climb to the top of the East Stand, Dad lagging behind as he curses smoke-filled lungs. At the entrance, I pause, transfixed and giddy. The pitch spread out below us, framed by the low roof and pillars, beguiling, seductive art with a soundtrack of clattering wooden seats as people found their places. Everything is new and vital in this world. The couple three rows ahead cover their knees with a blanket and break out the sandwiches and flasks. The man sneaks a furtive nip of something stronger into the cups.

Then the noise. Echoing around the rusting girders from all sides, ebbing and flowing in time with the game. Deafening, frightening, exhilarating. I had no experience of the world at 11 but I was certain there was nothing on earth like this feeling. I kick every ball. I learn to throw my hands in the air when Spurs score, to look around and share the moment with total strangers. For two hours there's nothing else, this is all that matters. I learn to be part of something.

My second match could have been the Cup Final. No loyalty points then. At the turn-stile we received a ballot card with a letter of the alphabet. At half time they announced the winning letters, each one greeted with a huge cheer from the lucky ticket holders. 'E' didn't come up. I wasn't disappointed because instinctively I realised it wasn't right, that others had a better entitlement, but I resolved that my time would come.

In 1967 Chelsea's bandwagon passed through my primary school playground. In those days the chosen method of showing allegiance or just gathering numbers for a quick kick-about was to place your arms across a mate's shoulders and march around, chanting the name of said activity. As others joined each end, the line grew longer. Movement was sideways, rather than a prepubescent conga line, so usually some altercations ensued as innocents got in the way. Many kids joined these lines purely for the purpose of inflict-

Art Turner
2012

Jimmy Greaves, always on the ball for Spurs

ing pain on their fellow schoolmates. On the Thursday lunchtime before the Cup Final, two lines started, one Chelsea and one Spurs. Chelsea's attracted more attention, then the herd effect came into play as the sheep and the psychos linked up with the vocal majority. Goebbels used similar tactics in the thirties. Within a few short moments, the playground was empty save for one extended line of over a hundred interlocked kids. And five Spurs fans, including me. The phalanx turned by the shelters, manoeuvred round the drinking fountains with surprising dexterity and came towards us, as solid as a Roman legion, a hundred pairs of eyes intent on their prey and the scent of blood in their nostrils.

What happened next wasn't pleasant. Suffice to say that reluctant on-duty teacher Mr Watson and the school caretaker will forever have my gratitude for stubbing out their sly fags and rushing from the back of the kitchens to rescue us. They all melted away, to next year become QPR fans as our other local team reached Wembley.

Amidst the scuffed leather and playground dust, I made a profound discovery. My faith was true. I am a Spurs fan.

With loving parents wary of allowing me to travel across London on my own, my subsequent trips were limited. One day I asked to go and Mum gave me a choice. She would take me that Saturday to see Tottenham play Burnley or I could go to Brentford on my own and she would buy me the Spurs shoulder bag that I desperately coveted. Being a serious child, I wrestled with this big decision all week. Eventually I took the sensible option: the bag would last and there would be other games, so Brentford it was. On the way home I learned from a crackly transistor that Spurs won 7-0 with a Greaves hat-trick including a rare header. From then on, my fate was set – there's being there or nothing.

You can't call my children gloryhunters. In their early twenties, they've known more downs than ups but they sit either side of me on the Shelf, close to where I stood boy and man since 1969. Granddaughter will be coming next year, she didn't take off her first Spurs shirt for a week. A new tradition. They know.

So much time, so many games but still my step quickens as I first glimpse the ground. Five minutes before kick-off, enclosed by expectation and the warm familiarity of this venerable old place, I lose myself in the noise, feel them close and there's nowhere in the world I would rather be.

After upheavals and dark times I wouldn't wish on anyone, I've lost touch with the people and places of my past but through it all there has been Tottenham Hotspur. The sole element of continuity from boy to man, son to grandfather, I have placed my fate in the hands of something over which I have absolutely no control, yet when passion is fulfilled, when Greaves glides goalwards, when Villa beats three at Wembley, Hoddle passes thirty yards or Modric drops his shoulder, there's nothing to compare.

When it finally gets too much, as I lie in my hospital bed, I want you to leave my bedside, kids, and go to the game. You know it's what I want. Then take my ashes one last time and after the final whistle scatter them amidst the feet of the tumult as you leave. Among the crowd is where I belong and that's where I will rest.

TONY BOXALL
Occupation: Retired detective/football blogger
Age: 55
Location: Hertfordshire via Tottenham
Spurs fan since: 1966-67
All-time favourite player: Jimmy Greaves
Blog: http://www.goodheightforagoalkeeper.com
Tony is a lifelong Spurs fan, now with time on his hands after retirement from Scotland Yard duty to pursue his dream of writing full time about football in general and Spurs in particular.

I HAVE been a Tottenham fan for as long as I can remember, and in the early days it was always about the walk, call it the 'Glory-Glory' Walk. I lived for the first ten years of my life in an N17 postcode, most of which was in Broadwater Road, a ten minute walk to White Hart Lane through Bruce Castle park. We moved to Wood Green when I was ten, and the walk became forty minutes, with a visit to the chip shop on the way home along Lordship Lane.

My football adventures before going 'down the Lane', consisted of playing in Bruce Castle park for hours on end during school holidays and weekends with my mates, pretending to be Jimmy Greaves dribbling through the defence, calmly rounding the 'keeper and passing the ball into the net Greavsie-style. If only the scouting system stretched to the local park!

We could hear the roars of the crowd from our house, where my mates and I had a profitable car-minding scheme on match days. Fans used to park in our road and walk through the park, down Church Road and across the High Road to the stadium. We used to ask if they wanted their cars looked after while they were at the game, and collected small change as payment when they came back to pick them up. Victory for Spurs brought richer rewards from happy fans. We took it in turns to sit on the kerb keeping an eye out while the others would go indoors and catch up with all the scores on *World Of Sport,* later sharing out the spoils.

To keep updated live with the Spurs score, we listened to the cheers from the ground and guessed the scorers. It is hardly believable now, and we could be on another planet. Those were the days when we used to queue up on a Saturday to get the evening paper – *Star, News* or *Standard* – to read an instant match report. It sounds prehistoric when we can now get updates all the time from a variety of sources; you can even watch live matches on your mobile phone! Reports are filed on line and people are blogging about the game almost as soon as it has finished. Keep up to date during the game on social networking sites if you want; how times have changed! Having said all that, there is nothing to compare with walking along with thousands of like-minded fans towards the magical Lane on a cold, rainy day or night to watch a game live. The pre-match rituals which we all cherish have changed as we have got older. This is my memory of the first time:

It was Wednesday April 12 1967, I was 10 years old. One of my Dad's friends had a spare ticket and as my father was working and couldn't go himself, his friend offered to take me. My Dad did however make me a wooden stool to stand on which I took to the game. I also had a wooden rattle – something tells me the Health and Safety people wouldn't allow those sort of things into a ground now!

The game was an FA Cup 6th round replay against Birmingham City. They were in the 'old' Second Division, Spurs were riding high in the First. The first game was a draw at St Andrews so I was taken to White Hart Lane to see the return.

On arrival, as became a regular routine, I was sat outside the Bell and Hare on the corner of Park Lane with a hot dog and a fizzy drink, my guardian for the night popping in for a swift half with his mates. I sat there with my wooden implements, wearing my bobble hat and scarf thinking I was the luckiest boy in the world. The noise, the buzz, it's still the same now, but as a young boy it felt like heaven to be even near to the ground, let alone about to be taken inside to watch a game.

We stood on 'The Shelf' in the East stand; I was perched against a metal crush barrier on my stool and looked out across the green baize pitch live for the first time. I had seen it on TV, but here I was, in person, watching my heroes up close and personal. There were over 52,000 people filling the ground that night, and the atmosphere was incredible. It was a different world and the most exciting place I had ever been to.

The team sheet in the programme was unbelievable, among the legendary names such as Pat Jennings, Mike England, Terry Venables, Alan Mullery and the, 'G men', Greaves and Gilzean, there was a colossus at left half, Dave Mackay. Possessing a fierce tackle, never-say-die attitude and demonstrating a fantastic example of leadership, Mackay was immense that night. It was a minor shock that Spurs had only drawn the first game. Iron man Mackay, back in business after twice breaking a leg, was not going to let a Wembley appearance slip by and drove the team on through the blustery conditions. Although memories dim after time, I can still open my mind's eye and see action from that game. Mackay picking the ball up after a crunching tackle, driving through the heart of the opposition before releasing one of the flair players. Extremely determined; a figurative giant amongst men.

Class showed through on the night, Spurs winning the game 6-0 to reach a semi final against Nottingham Forest. My hero, Jimmy Greaves scored two goals; Venables also got

Dave Mackay lets Billy Bremner know who's boss at The Lane in 1967

a brace, whilst Gilzean and Frank Saul completed the rout. Spurs won the semi and got through to the final where they beat Chelsea 2-1 to win the trophy, all made possible in no small way by the remarkable influence of Mackay.

Dave Mackay was one of the greatest players I have seen in a Spurs shirt. I only saw him live when he was coming to the end of his Tottenham career, having helped them to 'The Double' in 1961, FA Cup again in 1962, and European Cup Winners' Cup in 1963 before the 1967 triumph. He, of course, missed the European final because of injury but all the players set out to win the trophy for him, playing with the Mackay spirit.

I started to go to games regularly after this first night and was privileged to see him a few times before he left for Derby County in 1968. The famous photograph of him grabbing Billy Bremner by the scruff of the neck is still one of my favourite sporting images and shows the 'don't mess with me' attitude he took on to the pitch.

There are lots of other memories over the years, the moaning at Jimmy Greaves for his lack of work rate (before he popped up with the winner in the last few minutes and became a hero again). The sight of Alan Gilzean in a match on New Year's Day creeping around the pitch after Hogmanay, but rising where necessary to glide the ball off his head for a sublime knockdown or glanced header into goal.

The immense Mike England, the work rate of Alan Mullery, and the sight of the original Welsh wizard, Cliff Jones, flying down the left wing. These are just some memories of that era. The rest of the years have been typical Spurs, consistently inconsistent but laced with hundreds of magical moments to cherish and to tell the kids, and any grandkids about.

As a boy, I regularly went to home matches and the odd away game. My mates and I used to get to White Hart Lane about three hours before kickoff and queue at the boys' enclosure entrance. Once inside, you made your way to your usual crush barrier in the Paxton Road end to stake your claim and wait for the ground to fill up and the match to start. As I got older, we moved to the Park Lane end but wherever you stood, a remarkable thing used to happen during the game. When there was a near thing or better yet, a goal, the crowd swept forward as one to the barrier at the edge of the pitch and filtered back after. You used to end up back in the same place; and wait for the next traverse along the terraces.

The queue on a Sunday morning for FA Cup tickets (even the Final), used to snake around the ground, but as long as you were there early enough you came away clutching the golden treasure that was entry to watch your heroes in the next triumph. I was lucky in later years; I had a job which enabled me on some match days to be on duty inside the ground. Being paid to walk on the red clay surrounding the pitch before the kick-off, and then watch the game is the ultimate in job satisfaction.

It all had to start somewhere, a Tottenham boy being part of the FA Cup adventure in 1967 set me off on the right foot and moulded me into the life-long Spurs supporter I am today. And I *still* get a buzz from that walk to the ground. The Glory-Glory walk.

HENK ZANDBERGEN
Occupation: Physiotherapist
Age: 55
Location: Leiden, the Netherlands
Spurs fan since: 1963
All-time favourite player: Dave Mackay
Website: www.fysioseghwaert.nl

Henk played for ten years as a full-back for amateur club, Leiden (UVS), and he won representative honours with the Dutch National Student team. Married to Yvonne, they have two football-daft sons, Lucas 14 and Marcus 12, and he often gets to the Lane and follows Spurs closely on TV.

I T'S a cold Sunday morning in February 2010 and I'm waiting in the Departure Hall at Amsterdam Airport. My flight to Stansted will leave in about one hour. I try to remember how many times now I was in the same situation, heading for England, London and White Hart Lane. It has to be more than ten. Today's match is a traditional one against Everton. I remember the excitement I felt eight weeks earlier when I found out the match had been changed to a 1.00pm Sunday kick-off. This meant I was able to hop across the North Sea and back in a single day. There will even be time for a pre-and-post match drink in the Bell & Hare and a quick visit to the club store. This is the how I like it best, just watching the match, a few beers around the Lane and some talking to strangers, but sharing the same passion and at the end of the day cheerfully suffering a sore throat from all the yelling.

I also had some time to think over how it all started – 48 years ago now, and still seeing it very clearly. It was the time that clubs like Real Madrid, Internazionale and Benfica ruled over Europe. These clubs attracted lots of fans in those days, but my attraction would come from a very different angle. It all grew from the moment of opening a pack of chewing gum I bought with my pocket money. Included in the pack were the pictures of Malmo FF, CF Barcelona and Tottenham Hotspur. I can still remember the smell of the gum.

I have always found the most appealing clubs in the world were those with a double name, and those you could detect from the name where they came from, at most the district: Heart of Midlothian, Vasco da Gama, Boca Juniors. In Holland club names are mostly abbreviations and acronyms, three letters, or names of Greek Gods. For some reason the name "Tottenham Hotspur" leapt out at me. I was immediately impressed, even though I had no idea what the words meant and where the team came from. For this small boy from Holland it sounded like something from a different world. Over here in the Netherlands you didn't have football clubs with such a name. T-o-t-t-e-n-h-a-m   H-o-t-s-p-u-r. The title rolled off this Dutch boy's tongue, little knowing that this was the start of a love affair that has stretched nearly half a century.

From the three pictures in the chewing-gum packet the one of Tottenham Hotspur was the most impressive and inspiring: it was the one of the team with the 1961 FA and League Championship Cup trophies. The famous Double team.

The picture was in black and white, but had been coloured by an artist. The grass was a deep green, the shorts dark blue, shirts very white, even the cockerel with the ball on the shirts was coloured. Standing out to my young eyes in the front row, in the middle , was Bobby Smith (later on I found out we shared the same birthday of February 22). On the back row on the far right: Dave Mackay. Both players had that "over my dead body look" in their eyes. From that time on I decided when playing football in the streets with my friends, I was Bobby in attack, or – when playing defence – Dave.

The years rolled on and I continued to follow the Spurs from a very long distance. Just a few times you could watch them over here in Holland on TV when they reached a Cup Final, or when they entertained a Dutch team. Rare articles in the newspapers were always small and tucked away on the page. English football was far, far away. Falling in love and staying in love with the Spurs wasn't easy. I was very young, and of course there was no travelling for me to London.

As I grew older nobody seemed to understand why I supported an English club. Dutch football was rising and starting to earn its place as a power in world football. But the name "Tottenham Hotspur" was sculptured in my mind. Even the European successes of Ajax and Feijenoord couldn't divert or distract me. Later on, I discovered how well Tottenham played during the sixties with their two FA cups, League Championship and the European Cup Winners' Cup. One certain player named Jimmy Greaves was also known in the Netherlands as a goalscoring machine and was mentioned with respect.

The link between me and Spurs stayed, during my studies in other cities. I became a member of a local football club with the same formation year: 1882. I even had, after too many beers, the exciting idea of inviting Spurs for the anniversary game in 1982, but I was too scared and shy to turn my thoughts into action.

In 1978 I bumped into Ossie Ardiles and Ricky Villa at the National Training Ground of the Dutch FA in Zeist, where I was training with my club. I was too overwhelmed to react or say anything. Once on a trip with the National Student Team to London I bought a Cockerel scarf at Lillywhites at Piccadilly Circus. For some inexplicable reason I never had the plan or the courage to go and see Tottenham Hotspur live.

Bobby Smith, Tottenham and England centre-forward, who filled a young Dutch boy's imagination at the start of a 48-year love affair that is continuing to this day

And then came the Internet. This meant I was able to fall in love with Spurs for the second time. The club opened itself for me and I was able to read, hear and see more and more about Spurs. From that moment I had the possibility to learn all about the club and get in contact with people with that same "deviation" and devotion. Here I also rediscovered my chewing gum picture, which I had lost. This also meant a match ticket came closer. Still it took me some years to cross the North Sea.

It was my best friend who, memorably, arranged my first trip to the Lane of my dreams. He and a few other close mates were getting tired of all my stories and boring them with dull – and for non-believers – very uninteresting facts about a football club I only knew by hearsay. And it was they who clubbed together to send me to White Hart Lane with the message that from now on I had to keep my mouth shut, and do the thing I was always too scared and lazy to organise for myself. They sent my wife with me – to ensure I was coming back to them with hard evidence.

Well, stepping into White Hart Lane for the first time was the third and most emotional time I fell in love with the club. Since 2006 I have visited the ground many times, mostly two or three times a year. But the first time is the one that still gives me the goosebumps all over. All the clichés people in Holland say about English stadiums proved to be true: old neighbourhoods with the stadium close to someone's backyard, pubs and stands just a few meters from the pitch crowded with unconditional supporters. In some strange way I felt right at home.

But most impressive of all was the team playing at that particular ground. It was the time that Spurs were beginning to get their pride back with some excellent players, attacking football and with a little Dutch touch from the manager, Martin Jol.

At first I was a little afraid my mythical feelings could be over, because I was only living with names and pictures from the past. Nothing was further from the truth. It only got worse, I was really infected now. I have never had such a feeling in any other stadium and I know I won't have that sensation with any other club.

I still think it is hard to explain, and I leave it so. Friends and family think I'm a little crazy, shake their heads. They know that it is harmless.

Here I am back at Amsterdam Airport with my reflections of a 48-year love affair. I'll be back again at White Hart Lane within two hours, and the nerves are starting to jump again. It is impossible to go every week or even every month, maybe that is why it gives me this excitement. I now know where Spurs come from and England isn't a different world anymore. And I know what "Tottenham Hotspur" means. T-o-t-t-e-n-h-a-m H-o-t-s-p-u-r.

Chewing gum isn't my thing anymore. The best one I had 48 years ago. I had the opportunity of supporting Barcelona, but because of a name I came up with a better alternative!

JOHN WATSON

Occupation: Insurance broker
Age: 55
Location: Home Counties
Spurs fan since: Childhood
All-time favourite player: Jimmy Greaves

Married with two children, John has always had a keen commercial eye (Betamax Video Recorders, Sinclair C5s). Hopeful of tapping into the green economy, he has approached TV's Dragons' Den with his idea of sustainable Pie 'n' Mash shops, incorporating electric eels. Failing that, his wife has promised to improve his carbon bootprint in an ecologically sensitive area.

INCLUDED in the post this morning was a leaflet asking me if I felt tired, frustrated and stressed, and offered the solution in the form of certain alternative therapies. I must say, I've got to hand it to direct marketers these days. How did they know I'm a Spurs supporter? With the punishment we've suffered down the years, no amount of Reiki, Shiatsu, Indian Head massage or even Rolfing (I had to look that up – it's soft tissue manipulation; not, as I guessed, making exaggerated breathing noises with wobble board accompaniment) would alleviate the mental torture we've had to deal with in the name of following The Lilywhites. After all, if you look at the accompanying illustration above you don't get many 25 year olds with a fizzog like that.

This all leads me to the obvious question, which my wife has uttered, increasingly forlornly, down the years: 'What made you support them, if they keep letting you down?'

The simple answer is, to plead the Ollie Reed defence, 'I don't remember.' An even simpler answer these days is that if someone like Piers Morgan supports the other lot, what would any right-thinking person do?

As a child of the sixties, literally not hippily, two influences coloured my life and have done so since. Sport and television. There was I thought no immediate family connection with Spurs, as my father was a rugby man, but Uncle Dan – my Mum's brother – later revealed he'd been on their books as a youngster.

Football was played at school, and became the all-consuming preoccupation. It was played, opportunistically, anywhere and everywhere, inside and outside the house, at school, on the way to school, and the return journey. It was, I suppose, inevitable that the pervasive influence of Spurs, riding high at that time, and with a genius in their ranks, made their indelible mark on an aspiring striker, keen to follow in the footsteps of James Peter Greaves.

Then there was someone called Ferguson. Not the BBC avoiding, hair dryer applying, trophy magnet knight of the realm, legend of Manchester red. No, I refer to the eponymous manufacturer of TV sets. The Ferguson Flight was our first television, laughingly described as a portable, this half ton behemoth became the portal through which I could follow my team, albeit on a limited basis, given the paucity of TV coverage of football in those days. It was truly the magic rectangle, and brought us Z Cars, The Arthur Haynes Show, Grandstand, Harry Worth and Spurs, in black and white versus Manchester United, in grey and white.

Growing up as the oldest of six children in the sprawling hinterland where North East London meets Essex, Roding Valley was so anonymous it was known only by some of its residents and London Underground cartographers. My mother, officially The Hardest Working Person Ever, augmented my father's income by working nightly 12 hour shifts as an NHS nurse and then reverted, by day, to mother and housewife, eschewing sleep, to iron, clean and cook for a family of three boys and three girls. This combination of difficult location, cost and a mother's natural reticence to allow her young son to journey alone to football, meant opportunities to watch my team in the flesh were extremely rare. This is my plea in mitigation for being an early armchair supporter.

Spurs were my team, and despite attending a school in West Ham territory, and being taught and coached by West Ham players, the late John Cushley and Bryan 'Pop' Robson, nothing would sway me from the Lilywhites.

The first big event I recall involving Spurs on the box was the 1967 FA Cup Final. I remember using pocket money to buy a newspaper, unusually, specifically because it had a special pull-out supplement dedicated to the final teams. I can even remember Pat Collins tipping Chelsea, and, fine journalist though he is, I have held that against him ever since. That '67 side contained most of my boyhood heroes. Jennings, Kinnear, Knowles, Mullery, England, Mackay, Robertson, Greaves, Gilzean, Venables, Saul.

Especially Greaves and Gilzean, the G-Men. It had to be that pairing. Greaves, the best striker this country ever produced and the epitome of cool in front of goal. A coolness that extended, notably, to goal celebrations, which were, invariably, in inverse proportion to the brilliance of the goal. A determination to return to the centre circle with the minimum of fuss juxtaposed with team-mates exuberant at the result of his genius. How that humble attitude contrasts starkly with the ridiculous, overblown, choreographed, embarrassment we see from lesser players today. As Jimmy often said, scoring was his job, so why get too surprised or excited when he did what was expected of him? A balanced response from a man who showed that self-same trait on the pitch, and appeared to make time stand still in front of goal. His goal tally for club and country sets him apart from everyone else.

Alan Gilzean, his striking partner, was the perfect foil. Tall, lithe and darkly featured, and to use the modern euphemism, tonsorially challenged, his physiognomy suggested more a disdainful sommelier at The Ritz than a First Division footballer. Perhaps it was his unruffled demeanour, and habit of resting on the post at corners that gave this impression. Naturally, defenders would be lulled into a false sense of security, for which they would pay seconds later, either directly or via his strike partner. He appeared languid in the extreme, and would make Berbatov look hyperactive. Yet he could do things with his head that other players could not manage with their feet. No wonder he had little hair, with all those flicks. Look up 'deft' in the Oxford English and you'll see synonym: Gilzean header.

Pat Jennings was like no other goalkeeper who had ever played in the English League. Skills developed on the gaelic football pitch meant one handed saves, especially from corners, were commonplace, and his athleticism combined with an unconventional shot-stopping approach meant he often appeared to defy the laws of physics, all with no fuss or histrionics directed at his fellow defenders.

Another favourite was Cyril Knowles. To my mind the best left back Spurs ever had, and a man who, at one minute could be flying in for a tackle that would make his contemporary, Ron 'Chopper' Harris wince, the next pirouetting away from opponents with breath-taking skill. I'm sure it's not an urban myth or my memory deceiving me that Cyril, in one particular game, on his own goal-line, dragged back the ball behind him, thwarting by a millisecond an onrushing forward, and clearing nonchalantly, to loud applause. He had the sweetest of left feet, and as with all left sided sportsmen, a natural elegance that made him several cuts above your average clogger of the period.

And then there was Dave Mackay. Barrel-chested Mackay belied his somewhat diminutive 5'7" and was a colossus of the game. It was not just Billy Bremner who was grabbed by the scruff of the neck by this Scottish superman, but the game itself. No wonder George Best regarded him as the hardest player he ever played against; and the bravest.

All led by Bill Nicholson, our greatest ever manager, for whom the spotlight was as welcome as a garlic festival in Transylvania. If Greaves was the apotheosis of humility on the pitch, Nicholson exemplified it everywhere else, producing brilliant teams along the way, and providing the template for subsequent managers to aspire to; sadly, to date, unsuccessfully (But we live in hope under Harry's magical baton).

When I did get to see live games, primarily courtesy of the largesse of friends and neighbours, the big game to be at in the sixties was Manchester United. Arsenal, save for Ian Ure's memorable match winning appearances on *Quiz Ball*, the precursor to *A*

The enigmatic Alan Gilzean, a perfect foil to the Artful Dodger Jimmy Greaves

Question Of Sport, did not particularly register in my childhood consciousness as rivals. No, it was Best, Law and Charlton who were the big draw, and I can still recall watching Best from the Old Boys Enclosure at the corner of the East Stand, as mesmerised as Joe Kinnear, who was doing his utmost to try to mark him.

I've seen some wonderful stuff at White Hart Lane since, but nothing will replace my childhood memories and the magic of the sixties, and the players who epitomised Spurs' traditions for good football, and followed Danny Blanchflower's dictum, that it is all about style, and winning in style. Not about winning alone, and there's the rub. We cannot win ugly, or pragmatically. It is not allowed. It is a tremendous burden, in these highly competitive days, and always has been. We HAVE to win in a certain manner. That is the glory element, and why great Spurs teams will always be remembered. Even Bob Wilson stated the best team he ever saw was the '61 double team. That's a generous comment from a member of another double winning side, but it shows that when we are good, and we win something, it is extra special, and underlines why we support the mighty Spurs.

Editor's note: John is graciously donating any money he makes from this Spurs Writers' Club publishing project to the Demelza Hospice Care For Children charity

GERRY COX

Occupation: Football writer
Age: 52
Location: London (Ealing)
Spurs fan since: 1967
All-time favourite player: Jimmy Greaves
Website: www.hayters.com

Gerry runs one of the UK's premier sports agencies, and as a football writer has had what he calls 'the privilege and sometimes the misfortune' to cover Spurs across 25 years. He is a long-time Tottenham fan who strives to show press box neutrality.

I WISH I could say I became a Spurs fan because of a Jimmy Greaves goal I saw.

I wish I could reel off the great goals I watched the great man score, like any star-struck young kid who started going to White Hart Lane in the sixties.

I wish I could pick a one-two-three of my favourite Greavesie goals and replay them in my mind as vividly as I saw them in real life.

But the truth is I can make none of these claims because I never saw my hero score for Spurs. Hard to imagine, I know, that you could be anywhere near North London in the 1960s and not see a goal from the greatest goalscorer the modern game has known.

I don't need to repeat the stats here – although I am more than happy to state that James Peter Greaves managed 266 goals in 379 games for Spurs, having hit 100 before his 21st birthday and 44 for England in barely half the games that it took Bobby Charlton and Gary Lineker to reach that mark.

No, my main memory of Jimmy Greaves in colour (as going to football was in those days of black and white television) is hearing the crowd roar as he scored while we walked away from the Lane. That was at the last knockings of a shocking 3-1 defeat by Manchester City, our bogey team. Four-nil down and fed up, Dad and I decided to call it a day and walk back to my Nan's a few minutes before the final whistle, so we could beat the mass exodus at the end. We'd barely hit Tottenham High Road when we heard Roar One – for a penalty. Moments later, as we stood frozen to the spot with our heads tilted, comic-fashion, back towards the stadium, we heard Roar Two, as the ball was put in the net with the minimum of fuss by Greavsie (we presumed).

We were right. By the time we got back to Nan's, who had my favourite cheese-and-

Picallili sandwiches waiting before Sam Leitch elaborated on the action from Goodison Park, the news ticked over the Grandstand printer that indeed, the full-time score was Tottenham Hotspur 1 (Greaves, pen), Manchester City 3.

Little did I know then that, 20 years later, I would be a sports reporter for the famous Hayters Agency, sending scoreflashes through to Grandstand from grounds up and down the country. My only concern that day was that I had seen another game without seeing a goal from the master – and it was to go on until that horrible day in 1970 when the news came through that Greaves had gone – sold in a swap deal with Martin Peters, who, fine player though he was, never roused much enthusiasm in me. His arrival, after all, meant I would never see Greavsie score for Spurs.

When I was a small boy Jimmy was the only man whose name I knew, apart from Dad, the odd uncle, and the Beatles – and of course everybody apart from High Court judges knew who the Beatles were. And pretty much everyone knew Greavsie, a man who needs no introduction from me to fellow Tottenham aficionados. He was the Wazza and Gazza of his generation, with Rooney's skill and Gascoigne's attitude. He played with a smile on his face. We even called our first cat Jimmy, because of the way it flicked a tiny plastic football around when we got it back from the pet shop. It made no difference when it emerged that he was a she – we re-christened her Jemima but still called her Jimmy.

Even then, I lived in blithe ignorance of what went on in the world of football for the first seven years of my life, not able to comprehend that the Tottenham team of my infancy were – and still are – considered by some of the finest judges in the land to have been one of the purest football teams ever.

The 1966 World Cup passed me by, and with it all the hoo-hah about Greavsie missing the final. My only memory of it was when my game of tag on the stairs with my sister was interrupted by the sort of sounds from my Dad that suggested something wonderful or terrible was going on in the living room.

I even missed out on the fact that Spurs beat Chelsea to win the Cockney Cup final in 1967, although I remember going to my first match, at Stamford Bridge, a few months later as Chelsea got their revenge.

Like so many boys, I recall being lifted by my Dad on to the crush barrier, and savouring the smell, the vividness and the incredible atmosphere of the game, played out in glorious Technicolor, rather than the monochrome of the TV set.

I can still name the line up from Big Pat Jennings in goal to little Joe Kinnear, Terry Venables and the barrel-chested powerhouse in midfield. "Who's that fat bloke, Dad?" I enquired innocently about Dave Mackay. My Dad soon put me right. Neither of us could have imagined that I would get to know them so well, many years later, in my career as a football writer, which is really a state of suspended 'fanimation'.

Jimmy Greaves, whose 491 career goals went unwitnessed by Gerry Cox

I was awestruck the first time I sat in big Pat's sleek Jag to interview the world's greatest goalkeeper, less so as I started writing a column with genial Joe when he was manager of Wimbledon, and thoroughly professional when I used to ghost a column for TerryVen.

And it was a labour of love to write the big interview with Dave Mackay for the Spurs Opus, the rather grandiose book that cost thousands and sold considerably less. Sitting at White Hart Lane with Dave and his lovely wife, Isobel, with Cliff Jones popping over every now and then, reminiscing about the good old days. I had to pinch myself that I was keeping the company of the men I watched when I was just a small boy.

And yet there was no Greavsie to talk to – and there never has been for me. I have trekked the Himalayas with Ian Botham, sat with Pele, interviewed Daley Thompson and Carl Lewis, even played in the same press team as Bobby Charlton – but I never got to meet Jim. I've spoken to him on the phone sure enough, back in the days when I worked at *Shoot* and Greavsie's Letters Page was one of the most popular features. Standing in for the regular hack, I would ring the great man to put a few readers' comments to him. I remember one reader thought Graham Taylor was getting a rough ride from the press after failing to qualify for the 1994 World Cup. Greavsie's response had so much effing and blinding in it, I had to remind him it was for a kids' publication. Typical Greavsie – didn't care a jot what he said, and all in good humour.

There was the well-documented darker side, too, and I had read all about his battle with the bottle. That was why he didn't like to do after-dinner speaking, and kept away from the big boozy nights that were among the annual highlights of being a young football reporter. When I became Chairman of the Football Writers' Association in 2002, my first thought was to find a way to honour Greavsie, who had astonishingly never won our Footballer of the Year award. It is the Chairman's prerogative to suggest someone special to receive the FWA's Tribute award for lifetime achievement, handed over at a glitzy annual bash at The Savoy. Jim was my first choice, but sadly declined on the basis that he didn't like to be at boozy bashes, when the drink was flowing. It was understandable, but nonetheless disappointing.

I did get the chance, however, a few years later, to celebrate something special with Greavsie and my Dad, my heroes. It was February 2010, around the time of Greavsie's 70th and my Dad's 80th birthdays. I got tickets for 'An Evening with Jimmy Greaves' at the O2 Arena, and Dad came up by train and riverboat, while I drove down from covering West Ham that afternoon. It could not have been better. I reckon the demography in the room that night was not too different to those early games against Chelsea and Manchester City back in 1968.

On stage, they were all there – big Pat, little Joe, Dave Mackay – even Chopper Harris and Martin Peters. And of course there was Greavsie, larger than life, telling stories and cracking gags with the perfect timing he always showed on the pitch, and us, his adoring fans, loving every minute. I would guess the audience composition was pretty much as it was back in the day. There were plenty of grey-haired old men and the handful of blokes of my age would have been boys when Greavsie was in his pomp. But we loved it, the trip down memory lane and a reminder of the days when the Cockerel crowed out loud and Spurs played the best football in the land.

Amazingly, within a year, Spurs had recaptured their reputation as the great entertainers, playing with a style and swagger that brought back Danny Blanchflower's famous words: "Football is about glory, it is about doing things in style and with a flourish, about going out and beating the other lot, not waiting for them to die of boredom."

Having lived through the dross of the 'Sugar years' I was lucky enough to cover Spurs as they thrilled once again, in Milan and Madrid, beating the Arsenal on their own patch, seeing off the Chelsea curse, and establishing themselves as the side to watch.

It is no coincidence that it all came about under the guidance of Harry Redknapp, a proper football man cut from the same cloth as Greavsie and the rest of our heroes of the 60s. Harry played with the great man and understands exactly what was – and is – special about our club. I was at a League Managers' dinner with him in May 2011, and I said, putting professional protocol aside: "Thanks for giving us back our Spurs."

And that is how it is again. I can take my kids to White Hart Lane, not only without shame, but in the expectation that we are going to see football the way it should be played, that we are going to be entertained, enthralled, excited and delighted – just like it was when I was a little boy.

COLIN SANSOM
Occupation: Real Estate Sales Consultant
Age: 51
Location: Auckland, New Zealand, via Enfield
Spurs fan since: 1969
All-time favourite player: Glenn Hoddle

Colin was born in Hackney and lived his formative years in Enfield. He now lives in New Zealand, which he believes gives his twin daughters a better, healthier lifestyle. Spurs remain in his soul and he keeps in touch thanks to extensive TV coverage and the web social networks.

HAVING spent the very early part of my childhood living in Tottenham, growing up within close proximity of White Hart Lane, coupled with a few Spurs-loving family members, I guess these influencing factors encouraged my pursuit and avid interest as a lifetime supporter of Tottenham Hotspur. I can recall that my initiation into the Spurs footballing fraternity would have started from about the age of nine years old, anything before then having escaped my memory.

A milestone that jogs one of my earliest childhood memories as a Spurs supporter was when, as a family, we had just moved to West Yorkshire from North London in 1969, which became our home until we returned back south two years later. The very first match that I attended as a Spurs fan was in January 1971, and not at White Hart Lane but at the daunting Leeds United ground at Elland Road.

I was fortunate enough to be invited to the match by the manager of a boys' borstal centre – and before you ask, it was coincidental and not related to any dubious past personal exploits. The borstal manager was a fanatical Leeds United supporter and he offered to take me to an upcoming Leeds-Spurs game.

For those who are mature enough or with memories that can stretch back that far, Leeds United during the 1960s and part of the 1970s were highly successful, under the driving management of the late Don Revie. Therefore I did not hold out any high hopes that my impending visit to Elland Road was going to produce a favourable outcome for we loyal Spurs fans.

On that memorable evening, to my delight and that of a small band of travelling Spurs fans, Martin Chivers – our best striker at the time following the departure of Jimmy Greaves – scored both goals to secure a stunning victory.

My cheering had to be muted because I was a lone Spurs supporter sitting among a crowd of despondent Leeds United fans. I had to suppress any post-match celebrations until I was well away from Elland Road or risk an onslaught from any disgruntled Leeds fans.

Later that year we returned back south – home to North London, where my dream of attending a soccer match at White Hart Lane at last became reality.

During that era it was almost unheard of having foreign players in an English team, and I can recall going to a soccer match when it cost just £1 to get into the Lane – financed by my early-morning paper round. I would have spare change for any post-match celebrations, which included buying a portion of chips and a copy of the *Evening Standard*, so that I could catch up with the rest of the football results as I made my way back home to Enfield.

In 1973 I was fortunate enough to watch my first cup final, when Spurs played Norwich in the League Cup Final at Wembley. My next door neighbour, who I discovered was also a keen Spurs fan, kindly offered to take me with his son to watch the game. That day finished memorably for we Spurs faithful thanks to Ralph Coates, who came on as a substitute and scored the only goal in the 72nd minute to clinch victory.

My adventures took me to New Zealand and a new way of life, but I did have the luxury during a spell living back in the UK to watch games from the directors' box at Spurs. It was a once in a lifetime opportunity that will never be erased from my memory. At the time I was working for a company in London that sponsored the Football League, and there were a limited number of VIP complimentary tickets that allowed us to watch matches at White Hart Lane in comfortable surroundings.

It was sheer bliss being able to watch games from the vantage point of a warm, comfortable carpeted room, particularly when it was bleak outside. The games were televised on huge TV screens within the lounge area, so there was no need to move from the comfort of your chair and at the same time you could embrace the atmosphere of the crowd. A few of the Spurs players, including I recall Garth Crooks and Mark Falco, ventured into the bar area after the match

There have been many great players who have graced White Hart Lane over many decades, and it's not easy to single out one above all others. However, I can vividly relate to Glenn Hoddle's performances in the period whilst I was living back in the UK during the 1980s. He was and is still regarded as one of the one most gifted midfield players of all time, a visionary, a two-footed genius whose sublime ball control was unique, possibly the greatest passer of a ball; a true Spurs legend. Ironically, Glenn was discovered by one of my other all-time favourites, Martin Chivers, who spotted him playing youth football.

By sheer coincidence, I had the privilege of meeting Glenn when he owned a sports shop close to our then home in Bishops Stortford just prior to returning to live in New Zealand in 1988.

The introduction and subsequent development of satellite television and the internet has shrunk the 12,000 miles separating the UK from New Zealand, and our remote

Martin Chivers, Spurs goal scoring hero who discovered Glenn Hoddle

group of loyal Spurs supporters are now able to watch most games in 'real time'. The only disadvantage is the 12-hour time difference, which varies slightly with daylight saving.

What a complete contrast to when I initially returned to New Zealand coming up 25 years ago. The only means for we Spurs fans to stay informed back then was scanning the back pages of our daily newspaper for a small entry that simply displayed the previous weekend's UK soccer results, nothing more, nothing less. At the time, as a Spurs fan living in New Zealand, one felt quite isolated. It was fairly demoralizing, and I must admit that during the 1990s, due to the lack of advancement in technology, I lost touch with what was happening in the world of soccer back home in the UK.

One of the main drawbacks of watching live soccer games here in New Zealand is the time difference. For example, during the English soccer football season matches scheduled for 3pm on a Saturday afternoon in the UK, equates to 2am on a Sunday morning here.

As uncivilised as it may appear, one does adjust to this unsociable viewing time of watching soccer games, which fortunately are scheduled during the weekend, so recovery time is permissible. The upside from a personal perspective is that the 2am viewing of soccer games on a Sunday is probably the only time during the course of a week that I am able to enjoy any tranquility, as I am often distracted by the demands of family life and in particular an understanding wife, Angelika, who has accepted my lifelong passion, lively (and lovely) twin daughters as well as two demanding dogs.

There is a hard core of Spurs fans throughout New Zealand, including a Tottenham Hotspur Football Club, which organises events for ex-patriots including those like myself, who have emigrated from the UK. A small segment occasionally meet up to watch a match at a designated venue in the centre of Auckland, usually at a fairly respectable sports establishment, which is well decked out with large flat screen TVs, and the serving of beverages is a compulsory requirement. Despite the 12,000 miles between us and the UK, there is still the same enthusiasm and passion here for following one's own team and the rivalry between opposing club supporters is just as feisty as back home.

One of the most memorable matches that we have watched here in New Zealand on the big screen in a public sports bar was when Spurs beat Chelsea 2-1 in the League Cup final in 2008.

I feared my intrepid journey of 21 kilometres from my home into Auckland city had been to no avail but fortunately my doubts were soon dissipated. We came back from a goal behind to beat Chelsea when Jonathan Woodgate headed home the dramatic winning goal in extra time. It was a day for double celebration. My wife and I discovered we were to become parents to our beautiful twin daughters. It doesn't get better than that.

Despite some of the disadvantages and inconveniences of living overseas, our loyalty and enthusiasm for following our beloved Spurs will never falter or diminish. Regardless of opinions of our rivals, Spurs have had a reputation for many years as being one of the most entertaining soccer teams in the Premier League. Long may it continue. Coys!

LORRAINE WILLIAMS
Occupation: Runs an office-cleaning business
Age: 50
Location: Hoddesdon, Herts
Spurs fan since: 1970s
All-time favourite player: Glenn Hoddle
Business email: Blitzzcleans@aol.com

Lorraine started sneaking up to the Lane in the early 70's, telling her Mum she was going swimming. She says: "Just love it – the buzz, the smell of the grass, there's nothing better. When my boys were young they did all the Micky Hazard soccer skills. I got to meet many players, and was lucky enough to help Ian Walker present the awards one year."

I COME from an area where you either support a good team or that other team. We had a few Chelsea supporters at school, and one boy was even eccentric enough to support Charlton Athletic. This was pre-Beckham, so Man United was not on the map. These were the days when pop stars were covered in glitter and wore make-up – and they were the fellers. I liked football and Suzi Quatro. I think my Dad thought he had finally got the son he had always wanted.

I definitely would not have called myself a girly-girl in those days. However, I had a really bad crush on a boy in my class who was in the local footy team and Spurs mad. He never wrote in his exercise books; he just elaborately engraved THFC into the covers, then rolled them up and hit people with them. The day he whacked me I knew it was love!

The boys always went up the Lane and to away games on the Spurs coach, and that is what I wanted to do.

One of the best moments of my girlie life was the day my special "he" said, "D'ya wanna come up the Lane on Saturday?" What magical words that melted my heart. I was floating, the happiest person in the world. I got my Nan to knit me a navy and white scarf and bobble hat, and I told my Stevie Perryman poster on the bedroom wall what had happened: "Oooooh, Stevie, I'm gonna see you in the flesh!"

It's hard to put into words thirty-something years on how excited I was, going to see Spurs play with the light of my life, and when we got there it was even better than I could have imagined. I cant remember who we played, if we won or lost. What has stayed permanently in my memory is the beautiful smell of the grass, the roar of the crowd and the pure excitement of it all.

That was all in the early seventies and I'd say that was the day I fell in love with Tottenham Hotspur. Fom following a certain somebody around I had found a greater love (not that I didn't love you-know-who anymore. Poor boy).

I remember there had been riots abroad and football hooligans home and away were making the wrong sort of headlines. My Mum said I couldn't go anymore, so I used to lie to her and say I was going swimming and sneak off up the Lane. I had a few female friends who would come with me to look at boys, while I concentrated on watching Mr Perryman run around. What lovely legs that bloke had, and thighs to die for. Oh yes, I really appreciated the finer points of the game.

The first time I went to an evening game with the floodlights on I cried my eyes out because it all looked so beautiful. I witnessed the arrival of Glenn Hoddle, and swooned at his exquisite skill. Supporting Spurs at that growing-up, hormonal time of my life was a very personal thing. I'd cry if they won, cry if they lost (obviously, I had not discovered the pub back then, which would bring on a whole new set of emotions).

The year Spurs were relegated I felt like somebody had passed away; you know that feeling when you wake up in the morning and it begins to sink in that something bad has happened but it takes a while to think what, like when you've crashed your car.

 It was back then when I also first remember getting abuse from the supporters of that other team, which made me even more dedicated to my boys. Of course next season we bounced back up, and along came Ricky and Ossie and things were looking good again under the baton of Keith Burkinshaw. Lots more emotional outbursts, and of course that Ricky Villa goal in the FA Cup final. I wasn't there but watched it on telly, followed by the brilliant day when we all went up the High Road to watch them parade the Cup. Oh yes, and by then I had discovered the pub.

Strangely, my partner of the last 26 years does not appreciate the beauty of Tottenham Hotspur. I have taught him that we do not like the red and white team, and that sticking his head round the door and shouting, "Can you hear the Gooners sing" is not a good idea. But he is quite happy for me to go off with the kids and my football friends to follow the Lilywhites.

Both of my sons have obviously been encouraged to support Spurs from an early age. I always enjoyed taking them up the Lane as youngsters, and now they feel they are taking me.

Things have moved on so much since my school-crush days watching Stevie, Glenn and the gang turning it on at the Lane. The whole attitude towards our children has changed,

Keith Burkinshaw, who brought Ossie Ardiles and Ricky Villa to Spurs

and we now encourage them to take part in sport and support them.

My boys did lots of Micky Hazard soccer skills over the years which were brilliant. I got to meet so many of the players, and even helped that brilliant goalkeeper Ian Walker give out the cups one year. I would like to think the boys enjoyed it too!

My boys used to go to the training ground at Cheshunt, which is something I never did. I regret it now, but I felt at the time it would spoil the magic seeing the players out of the context of the Lane.

I feel very proud to have been asked to write my piece for this book, giving a woman's eye view of my beloved Spurs. There are lots and lots of Yiddettes, and I like to think I am speaking for many of them who have enjoyed my kind of experiences following a very special club.

Yes, I have mellowed from those days when I used to cry in victory and defeat, but I am still very passionate about Tottenham Hotspur and still shout as loud and enjoy looking at the legs and thighs of great athletes. I also like to think I now understand the finer points of the game, and I know and and appreciate that with Tottenham I am seeing the Beautiful Game played to its highest level.

I was going to say I an not as emotional as when I was a kid, but I do still stand there with tears running down my face when the team have touched peaks of perfection under Harry Redknapp.

I am really lucky, because one of the companies I work for in my 'blitz clean' business has three season tickets, which I get to use quite often. I have another dear friend who takes me when he can.

Now I have started taking my daughter, but it's all so different for her from "my day." No roughing it with the boys. No slipping off behind her mother's back to watch the team play. No getting whacked with the rolled-up school exercise book.

But she loves it all the same, which is the most important thing. She knows the joy of being a member of the Yid Army.

And the grass still smells just as beautiful.

IAN BULLEN
Occupation: Volunteer worker
Age: 48
Location: Devon
Spurs fan since: 1978
All-time favourite player: Steve Perryman

Ian was fit and mobile for many years, but everything changed for him in tragic circumstance in 2004 when he broke his neck during a night out in Plymouth. Permanent paralysis means many aspects of Ian's life have changed in the most challenging of ways, but his passion for Tottenham still burns brightly.

MY introduction to Tottenham Hotspur began on May 3 1978 when Spurs played an end of season friendly against Truro City, local to me down in the West Country. Spurs had just gained promotion back to the top tier of English football after spending the 1977-78 season in the old Second Division.

I was a shy, skinny 14-year-old at the time who happened to live over 300 miles away from this mesmeric place they called White Hart Lane, but I made a promise to myself on that warm, spring Cornish evening to pursue this new feeling of excitement and fervour.

However, this chapter is not about 1978, but another game that was played 27 years later, on May 14 2005. Come with me back to a nightmare time in my life ...

I have just spent eight months at Salisbury spinal unit in Wiltshire after stupidly breaking my neck on a night out in Plymouth. During this ill-fated incident, a vertebrae at the base of my neck had dislocated and completely severed my spinal cord. This, I am informed by the medics, means that I am now paralysed from the shoulders down and totally reliant upon nursing care for the rest of my life.

Coming to terms with this life-changing scenario will not be easy, but despite this, friends and family remain positive and upbeat.

At the beginning of my rehabilitation, I am completely oblivious to the outside world. Even the surrounding area seems dreamlike and delusional for the first few days, but thankfully this subsides and I am now able to focus on reality and the prospect of moving forward.

My dedication to Tottenham Hotspur has remained resolute since 1978 and this addiction to the Lilywhites has always been shared with my best pal Andy. Our sons have also been carefully primed and nurtured to follow this same path before my accident, so it seems completely natural to resume this passion as soon as possible.

During my stay in hospital, I have managed to keep in touch with the comings and goings at White Hart Lane through conversations with the hospital staff, my loyal mate Andy and a small digital radio, that I have constantly tuned into Radio 5 Live.

I remember anxiously listening to the live commentary of the topsy-turvy North London derby on Saturday, November 13, 2004 when Arsenal came out on top after a scintillating nine goal thriller.

Another moment of radio torment on Tuesday January 4, 2005. Spurs travelled to Old Trafford to play Manchester United, but were denied a rare and historical victory when the officials failed to notice that Pedro Mendes's shot had clearly crossed the goal-line.

However, this audio contact is not enough. I am hankering to savour the pre-match atmosphere at White Hart Lane again. The smell of fried onions and cheap cigar smoke. The euphonious sound of "Glory Glory Tottenham Hotspur." And to sense that auspicious bond and unity that all Spurs fans have for one another.

Unbeknown to me, good things were going on behind my back and my reawakening will soon occur on the last day of the 2004-05 Season against Blackburn Rovers.

A wheelchair/carer ticket has been purchased on my behalf in the disabled section of the South Stand and specialised transport between Salisbury and North London has also been secretly arranged.

To cap things off, a genuine Spurs-supporting nurse from the spinal unit will be escorting me on this momentous day. This was Elaine, who is clearly in charge of all the other nursing staff at the unit, but despite this she always finds time to chat with me, and to tell me how she remembers the buzz and excitement of going to White Hart Lane as a little girl with her father.

Finally, Sunday May 14 arrives and I awake earlier than normal with a mixture of excitement and trepidation. There are so many more things to think about now.

How will I cope trying to manoeuvre my chin-control wheelchair on the bumpy pavements and around the throng of traffic and supporters on the High Road?

How will the other Spurs fans perceive and receive me?

Before and after each game previous to my disability, Andy, myself and a few pals would always have a beer, or two in the 703 Club. This bar is opposite White Hart Lane stadium, so this perfect location will be our meeting place with Andy and the boys on this momentous day

It doesn't take long to confront my first obstacle, the threshold to the main entrance to the 703 is much too high. I try time and time again to get inside, but with no success.

Fortunately, some fans who are inside, see me struggling and immediately walk over to

Ian Bullen, photographed on a visit to that "mesmeric place" White Hart Lane

the doorway and grab hold of my large, heavy wheelchair and lift me inside.

This expression of solidarity makes me feel much easier, and moments later we are all joining in with the pre-match singing and merriment.

After a while, I feel a tap on my shoulder. I slowly turn my head to be greeted with a familiar beaming smile, and a opening line that I will never forget:

"You fucking ignorant bastard, I have been waving at you for the past 10 minutes and you can't be bothered to wave back!"

It's an old friend, Paul. Some might say that this is not the most tactful welcome to make to a person who is tetraplegic, but for me his joking approach is perfect.

Any barriers of silly paranoia that I have created in my own mind are instantly diminished and I am now prepared to savour this special afternoon.

At 3:30 p.m. Elaine and I leave the 703 and make our way slowly to the iron gates on Bill Nicholson Way. I feel quite privileged to be entering the stadium in this way, carefully navigating my wheelchair alongside the glamorous collection of Mercedes and Ferraris.

This momentary feeling of grandeur soon evaporates on reaching the disabled entrance, where we are carefully frisked for any weapons of mass destruction.

Once we are deemed safe to continue, we pass through the darkened tunnel that takes us down to the corner flag at the southwest corner of the pitch.

The noise and light at the end of this tunnel completely overwhelms me. I am finally back at my spiritual home, the place that has been graced by the studmarks of Blanchflower, Jones, White, Greaves, Mackay, Mullery, Perryman, Chivers, Hoddle, Ardiles, Gascoigne, Ginola and countless others.

On entering the disabled area I feel like the new boy at school again. In reality, other wheelchair users pay little attention to me, but my embarrassing parking skills draws the attention of the Tottenham stewards.

At last, I am settled, to finally absorb every aspect of this divine moment. The away fans are directly behind me, but nothing is going to spoil this experience. A second wave of emotion engulfs me and I am now desperately trying to stay in control, but my eyes are starting to well up and very soon large salty teardrops are racing down my face.

Without any words, the lovely Elaine leans forward and dabs my tear-stained eyes as the players walk out onto the pitch.

That match against Blackburn Rovers will never be remembered for football reasons, an uninspiring scoreless stalemate that was almost forgotten by the time we reached the M25. But that afternoon in North London was all about embracing a passion for a special football club. An association of all types, Black, White, Jewish, Christians even atheists. Able-bodied, disabled, young and old, all brought together to be able to share this powerful experience and rejoice, regardless of your circumstances.

Spurs 'Til I Die.

ADDY OLUBAJO
Occupation: Director of Human Resources
Age: 47
Location: London via Liverpool
Spurs fan since: 1980
All-time favourite player: Glenn Hoddle

Addy 'emigrated' to London from Merseyside in the early 1980s and carried on his devotion to Tottenham despite living within walking distance of 'the enemy' at Highbury.

A LOT of people have questioned why a born and bred Merseyside lad decided to turn his back on what was in the 80s the greatest team in the world – Liverpool – to go and support what was then a so-so team in North London – and I don't mean Arsenal, but the famous Tottenham Hotspur.

Well the events in the 2011-12 season surrounding John Terry and Louis Suarez and the appalling abuse of a black Oldham player at Anfield put this into perspective.

As a young black football-loving lad growing up in Liverpool, I can tell you neither Anfield nor Goodison Park is the place to spend your Saturday afternoon watching a football game if you are of a certain colour.

I can put up with abuse from opposing fans – but from your own supporters, I really detest that. I read an article written by a black journalist who happens to be a Chelsea fan commenting on the John Terry saga. He started going to the Bridge when he was younger and tolerated a lot of racial abuse among his own supporters until he stopped going to watch the Blues.

For me it was different. It was something I would not tolerate, and it did not matter to me whether Liverpool were the most successful club in the land at the time. I made the decision not to support the club, and besides Red is not my favourite colour.

Whether it was the right decision at the time I don't know. As soon as my Scouse friends discovered I was a Spurs fan my life became hell as Tottenham could not beat Liverpool, in fact the last time we recorded that feat was in 1912, the year the Titanic sunk. The Scousers were also quick to remind me when Liverpool trashed Spurs 7-1 at Anfield. I tell you now that was the worst day of my entire life. But something I had and the Scousers failed to see was my vision by keeping faith in Spurs – and I've never regretted it.

Why Tottenham I hear you say. Well I always had the inclination that somehow I was going to end up in London and I think it was actually the Cup final in 1981 that finally sowed the Cockerel in my heart, and I have not looked back since. One thing I cannot be accused of is being a glory hunter, otherwise I would have started supporting the enemy even though they had a number of prominent black players at the time. But, like I say, Red is not my thing.

My first appearance at the Lane was in April 1983, when Spurs were playing Ipswich Town. I recall we won one-nil with the goal scored by Glenn Hoddle. I remember walking into the ground and kind of instantly felt at home. The fans were wonderful, warming and welcoming. So different to the reception I used to get at Anfield.

It was a day I will never forget.

I also recall that the East Stand at the time was all standing, and the elderly man standing next to me had his young grandson with him. Unfortunately the boy could not see the game and the grandfather asked if I would mind carrying the little lad on my shoulders, so that he could watch the match. I was happy to do this, and at the end of the game the grateful Granddad pushed a £20 note into my hand!

From that day onwards. the Lane became my shrine and it was the place to find me every Saturday at 3:00pm. The traditional Saturday as it's known. Four years later I was to witness the first of the glory years that climaxed with the UEFA Cup Final second leg at the Lane. There I was tucked at the very top of the old South Stand, and I almost tumbled to the bottom row when Graham Roberts squared the game with that glorious shot that ripped into the net, Then Tony Parks saving a penalty indicated that I had definitely made the right choice in choosing Tottenham as my team.

Little did I know when I eventually moved to London to live that I had chosen to settle down in enemy territory – Highbury to be exact! I had escaped the Red of Liverpool only to find myself surrounded by the Red of the Arse. It is true to state that at that time many black people in London supported the Gunners, and it didn't take long for me to find out about the deadly rivalry between both teams.

Initially in the early eighties Spurs were the bigger team and I witnessed them beating Arsenal 5-1 in the League. I am also proud to recall that I was on the Highbury North Bank when Spurs recorded their last victory at the old home of the Gooners.

My troubles started when the balance of power began to shift and Arsenal emerged as the dominant team in North London. My life became a living hell with all those Gooners around me, be it in the neighbourhood, University, at work – wherever I turned. You will recall the epic battle in the Milk Cup semi-final that went to three games. Boy oh boy, did I suffer in the final game when we lost. At the time I was still at uni and it could be said that half of the students at the time were committed Reds.

Younes Kaboul, put the finishing touch to an eight-goal thriller against Aston Villa

But, as they say, revenge is a dish best served cold. That brings me on to April 1991, and my first Wembley experience. If I was a betting man this could have been the day I cleaned out the bookies. Two weeks prior to the game I had a flash in my dream of a score line of 3-1 to the Spurs. I remember that day as the most nervous of my life, I could not sleep or eat for weeks as there was a lot at stake. For those of us living in North London it was as if war was about to break out. I was flying the lone blue and white flag on a street of red and white.

I still had a premonition that we were going to win, yet deep down could not believe it as no one gave us a chance. According to the pundits all Arsenal had to do was show up. Making my way up to Wembley all I recalled seeing was a sea of red and white flags until I made it to King's Cross, where I was joined by more Spurs fans. The banter between the rival supporters was funny without being malicious.

On reaching Wembley my nerves were so fragile I felt I would collapse at anytime. The atmosphere was unbelievable, and by the time the game started my heart rate was running at almost 600 bpm, How I managed to stay alive was beyond me!

Then came that moment, the magic moment, a free kick to the Spurs and that man, yes Paul Gascoigne, took the ball and placed it and the rest is history. A fantastic goal to the Spurs, with David Seaman beaten all ends up. By the time Gary Lineker scored the second goal all we Spurs fans were going crazy. The Gooners pulled one back but then Gary scored our third goal to make my dream come true.

After the final whistle even the players were so delirious they came back out to celebrate with the fans. Two hours after the game finished we were all still at the stadium, still celebrating and wondering how we managed to pull this one off.

Yes, finally we had beaten the auld enemy and better still we went on to win the Cup that year. That was probably the proudest moment of being a Spurs fan for me. To date.

No matter what, once you have nailed your sail to the Tottenham mast there is no going back. I have managed to pass on the bug to the rest of the family, and am now from a household full of Spurs supporters, which brings me to another proud moment. You will recall the 125th Anniversary game against the Villains. It was extra special for me because my eldest daughter was lucky to be chosen as a mascot for the game, which turned out to be memorable for Ramos's last game in charge and the beginning of the Rednapp era. The Villa fans sang "Happy Birthday" when leading 3-1 and Younes Kaboul brought the game back to 4-4 with the last kick of the game. What a night.

More pride for the Olubajo family came when my youngest, Michael, was also chosen to be a mascot for the January 2012 third round FA Cup tie against Cheltenham.

I am sure there is more to come for another chapter, another book. So stay tuned.

Thank you Tottenham for making this Scouser – this black Scouser – feel at home.

IAN LANGLEY

Occupation: Local Government
Age: 43
Location: Hertfordshire
Spurs fan since: 1980
All-time favourite player: Glenn Hoddle
Website: www.facebook.com/graham4roberts

Ian is a Local Government manager working on projects with Tottenham Hotspur FC to improve the life chances of children and young people in the locality. He also boasts a fine collection of Spurs memorabillia and on occasions has turned out for the Spurs Legends side.

THEY (whoever they are) say that you end up returning to your roots. I was born in London and at the age of five moved down to the south coast with my mother and sister. I recall following Liverpool at that age because everybody else was. Sounds strange now, but that's how it was in an era when the Reds were winning everything in sight under the direction of manager Bob Paisley, and with the likes of Kevin Keegan and Terry McDermott in full flow. During this time I was drawn towards Spurs but never really knew why, possibly because I recall vividly seeing Hoddle wearing that wonderful Admiral strip in one of the football magazines. I stopped following Liverpool for two reasons: first, that it became tedious supporting a team that I had no real connection with, and second, I had discovered that my whole family were Spurs fans. It wouldn't have felt right following anyone else.

Although I grew up on the south coast my parents and grandparents and extended family hailed from North London. In fact one of my late mother's abiding memories was seeing the double winning Spurs team parade past her flat in Fore Street during the victory procession in 1961. Given the history there was an inevitability that I would end up following Spurs and of course I did, making up for the recalcitrance of my younger years.

I recall collecting posters from *Shoot* magazines and sending them off for the players to sign. In 1982 I wrote to Steve Perryman asking for his advice and to his credit and to reinforce my hero worship he wrote back on note paper which I have kept in an album of clippings and autographs. I also remember writing to Jim'll Fix It asking if I could fulfil a dream by training or playing with my heroes, and like so many that did I heard nothing. Little did I know at the time that some thirty years later that dream would be fulfilled.

I'll never forget my first visit to White Hart Lane, because it very nearly didn't happen.

The game I had arranged to see was Spurs v. Bruges on November 7 1984, which was also the 40th birthday. of my step-father, Rod. Tickets to see Tottenham play, the perfect present. Back then there was no internet and so I sent a cheque off and excitedly awaited the arrival of my tickets. I waited and waited and started to become anxious when three days prior to the game they still hadn't arrived. My anxiety turned to nausea when I saw the chewed corner of what would have been the tickets resting where the post would have fallen. Our eight week old puppy, Cindy, had a lot to answer for! I phoned the club and explained what had happened, and they arranged for me to pick up duplicates, which were more like pieces of paper rather than tickets, with the stand and seat number on them. I still have these today.

The journey to Tottenham took a couple of hours. I remember stepping out at Seven Sisters and seeing and feeling the hustle and bustle of those making their way to the ground. The High Road was vibrant with activity and I recall the chill of the evening and the pace of the walk to the ground warming me up. Then it hit me, the glare of those floodlights. This was it, I had arrived at MY club. Sure, I'd seen us on the television and even seen us play Southampton at The Dell, but to be within seeing, hearing and touching distance of this magnificent stadium with all its history was so, so special.

We made our way to our seats having brought a programme outside. The view from the newly constructed West Upper was magnificent, and when the players made their way onto the pitch the floodlights against that all white strip made them glow like jewels in the night. I could barely contain my excitement, the show was about to commence and I knew I'd never forget what I was about to see.

The irony was that nearly thirty years on and even well before now I really only remember three aspects of the match itself that concerned two players, Graham Roberts and Micky Hazard. Looking back I can't recall whether at the time I realised that the team I watched in the November was pretty much the same one that had won the Uefa Cup only a few months previously, although I'm sure I must have. Now of course the history slots into place as well it should. What I do recall though is watching Micky Hazard twisting and turning away from players as if they weren't there. There he was in this long sleeved Lilywhite shirt holding the scruffs of his sleeves. Why I remember him holding the sleeves is beyond me but I do!

The other reason for remembering Hazard and Roberts is that they both scored. Clive Allen also scored but for some reason I don't recall his goal or at least not as vividly. If memory serves me well Micky scored a curler with his left foot from the right side of the box at the Paxton Road end, and then Roberts scored a goal that for me at that age, at my first game defied belief. I've since watched his goal on the internet and I don't think the film does it justice.

As I sat there looking down the ball was cleared from the Bruges end and I remember watching it come out of the area. Robbo was running towards it and I said to Rod, who was sat next to me, 'he's going to hit this, he's going to hit it!' He didn't just hit it, he hammered

That's me, Ian Langley, with my 'fixer' pal Graham Roberts and the Uefa Cup he did so much to help win for Tottenham in 1984. Robbo is a Lane Legend.

it with his right boot. The shot was unstoppable and I knew that from the moment it left his foot it was destined for one place only and that was the top corner and in it went. I was ecstatic, it couldn't have been any better. We won the game 3-0.

I left the game vowing that one day I would have a season ticket, no matter what it took. I even chose a University that was within travelling distance so that I would be closer to the Lane. I became a season ticket holder in the 1996/97 season and as you'll know things weren't great for a few years around that time, although I've always felt privileged to be sat in that stadium watching my team play.

I went to the odd away game but not on a regular basis and then by chance I met a fan who travelled away frequently and who suggested I should join him when he did. What he didn't tell me was that a regular traveller on those away journeys was none other than Graham Roberts. It was surreal sharing a mini bus journey to Burnley for the second leg of the Carling Cup semi final with him and to take his money at three card brag topped it all! We even watched the UEFA Cup Final on DVD on the way up, unbelievably with the captain of the side that won it!

My friendship with Robbo grew from that point and although Jim couldn't fix it for me, Robbo did. He enabled me to debut for the Spurs Legends side in Exeter on July 19 2009. Just as I'll never forget my first trip to White Hart Lane, I'll never forget Robbo fixing it for me.

I'll also never forget Steve Perryman telling me I was coming on up front for Brooksy (Garry Brooke) at half time! Things developed from that point on and we did some signing sessions for fans that also included the likes of Micky, Ossie and Ricky as well as Keith Burkinshaw. Thanks to Graham I also went on to make a few more Spurs Legends appearances and through him have also got to know Micky Hazard very well, who I see on a regular basis, and have the privilege of collaborating with him on his football memoirs

I've been fortunate to support a club like Spurs. I've travelled home and away and made some good friendships in that time. I've seen us win Cups and suffer losses I'd prefer to forget, and I've become good friends (and the occasional team mate) with two players who were there with me at that very first game even though they never knew it.

I've always said that if the fairytale of my journey with Spurs ended tomorrow I'd have no regrets and would savour every moment, but somehow I feel this is a story that will continue for some time to come – particularly as my two boys, Joshua and Adam, are following the family tradition and are supporting the best club in the land. The future's bright. The future's Lilywhite.

DANIEL WYNNE

Occupation: Banker and Spurs commentator
Age: 41
Location: Chigwell, Essex
Spurs fan since: 1975
All-time favourite player: Ossie Ardiles
Website: www.tottenhamtt.org

Daniel's Spurs-mad Dad first took him to see Tottenham play when he was five, and he's been going ever since. For the last 11 seasons he's been the Lane commentator, and is a Trustee of the Tottenham Tribute Trust. He loves his total involvement with the Club.

So, where did it all begin? I had an idyllic childhood. We lived in middle-class suburbia in north London and I was happy as Larry with my Mum and Dad. My much older brother had by then moved out as he went to uni at Cambridge, and my sister moved out to live in Israel fairly soon after I was born, so it was just me, Mum and Dad, plus the au pair. In fact, we had got through a few au pairs, all from mainland Europe but hopefully they didn't move on as a result of me! Perhaps that is where my love of European competition came from, but more of that later.

I was young but I remember as clear as anything that Dad used to disappear on a Saturday around lunchtime and come home near supper time, sometimes in a good mood, other times less happy but where did he go? What was this thing called football all about? Why wasn't I able to go with him? After all, I was nearly five and at big school so surely I could go with him, couldn't I?

With the benefit of hindsight I can see now that my Dad may have wanted to protect me from the often less than pleasant surroundings of Division 1 football of the mid 1970's, but I was having none of it. Nor was my Mum, who clearly wanted Saturdays to herself. So eventually I was able to join my Dad and make my first trip to what has since become a place that is so very close to my heart.

August 16 1975 was the date, just short of a month before I turned five. The events of the day are etched in my mind. I won't ever forget it, and on many occasions since then I've never forgiven my Dad for taking me!

My Mum packed a bag of goodies for me to take in case I was bored. Bored? Why would I be bored? I was going out with Dad to football, I couldn't possibly be bored at a place he went to so regularly.

We drove in his blue and white (naturally!) Hillman Avenger the six or so miles from Cockfosters to Tottenham. I didn't quite know what to expect, but as we approached the area I was told to look out for the floodlight pylons in a kind of "can you see the sea yet?" way. I could, but I had no idea what they were or why I was looking for them. What did those four towers have to do with football?

We parked and we walked for a while along with a shifting crowd towards the pylons. I had never seen so many people in one place. Middlesbrough were our opponents on the opening day of the 1975-76 season and it was also the opening day of the rest of my life.

I recall people shouting at me on the street. "Programmes" … "Roasted peanuts" … "Hot dogs and hamburgers" … "Wear your colours" were among the shouts aimed my way. It scared me a little. Why were they shouting at me? I hadn't done anything wrong. Dad was ok with it, so that reassured me that I wasn't in danger!

We turned the corner and in front of me were the steps to the old west stand, with the big Tottenham Hotspur sign looking down at me. Streams of people wearing navy blue and white walked up the steps and I was about to join them. Dad held my hand and looked at me with a proud smile, and in a way not too dissimilar of a father to his daughter just before walking her down the aisle, he asked me, "Are you ready?" I didn't need to be asked twice. Yes, I was ready to take Spurs as my lawful wedded club.

We climbed the steps, we went through the turnstiles and we were in. Older readers who are familiar with the old layout of the ground will know that Block J of the main stand was central and just by the Directors' box. Our brown, wooden seats were waiting for us there.

It is etched on my mind that as I came into the arena, with the lush pitch in front of me, I feared I would fall out of the stand! I held on to my Dad for dear life. Once seated I took it all in. I looked out across the stadium and out onto the pitch. I liked what I saw. I liked what I heard and what I could feel and smell.

The record books tell me that 25,502 people were at that game, but it felt like millions to me. The noise seemed to draw me in. The roar when the Spurs team took to the field nearly deafened my young ears but it was nothing to what would follow when Steve Perryman scored the only goal of the game.

I sat open mouthed watching the game, listening to the sound of the crowd, trying to decipher the words of the songs that were being sung. The men near where I was sitting were angry sometimes and shouted at some of the players. I hoped they weren't going to shout at me.

Steve Perryman, who scored the winner in Daniel Wynne's first match

As quickly as it started, the game was over. The 90 minutes flew by and I loved it. I was hooked. I was in love and I knew that I wanted more. I was to get my wish as my fifth birthday was less than a month away and my Dad managed to buy me a season ticket near his seat and that was that. I've been lucky enough to have had a season ticket ever since.

A lifelong devotion, or some may call it illness, began on that August day at the impressionable age of "nearly 5". I've two boys of my own now. Josh is 17 and Max is 14. They both come to games with me and I had that same proud feeling that my Dad had when I took them to their first games.

My Dad sadly gave up going to Spurs in 1991. His last game was our FA Cup Final victory v Nottingham Forest. He was becoming disillusioned with the amount of money in the game, both for fans and for players.

In his day he went all over Europe to watch Spurs, so I just couldn't understand how he could stop. At the age of 41, as I now am, I admire him for sticking to his principles and hope that in the future, I wont be forced to follow his lead.

Dad died in July 2006. I don't have many regrets in life but I so wanted him to come to a game with my boys, so the three generations of us could be at a game together. He didn't oblige. I managed to persuade him to go to the Bill Nicholson memorial service at White Hart Lane but for some reason he pulled out on the morning of the service. That was the closest we came to all being at the stadium together.

He told me that he was proud of the fact I was involved with the Club, and loved seeing me on TV and hearing me on the radio talking about the Spurs related matter of the day when called upon by the media to give a reaction. I was delighted that he was so proud.

It is safe to say that Tottenham Hotspur is an important part of my life. I have been commentating on THFC's home games for 11 seasons and am a trustee of the Club's Tribute Trust charity, which helps our former players in later life. It is no lie to say that I still get the same buzz of excitement when I take my seat in the stadium today as I did all those years ago.

Like my Dad before me I have been to see Spurs all over Europe. and I proudly took my boys for our first away game in Europe together against Real Madrid in the 2010-11 season (Don't get me started on Peter Crouch's early red card!).

Who knows what the future holds, but back in August 1975 I somehow knew that I wanted Tottenham Hotspur to be a part of my life and I'm delighted that it has been, and I am proud to have my regular place in the gantry as the match commentator.

I do a full live, 90 minute commentary for every home game. It is heard live in the executive lounges and boxes and the games are recorded on to DVD and they form part of the management team's analysis, plus the FA receives a copy too. I adhere to the motto – *fail to prepare, prepare to fail.* That could also be the Tottenham motto under Harry!

 # 21. Gazza and a pregnant pause

LEZ DORKEN

Occupation: Teaching assistant; studyng for BA in education
Age: 40
Location: Welwyn Garden City, Herts
Spurs fan since: 1982
All-time favourite player: Glenn Hoddle

Lez, who assists teachers of childen with special needs, comes from an Arsenal stronghold, but rebelled against family tradition and chose to support Spurs. This leads to what she describes as "interesting family discussions"!

COMING from a whole family of Arsenal fanatics (and I do mean a whole family) and being the rebellious child I was, meant only one thing... I would support Spurs! Looking back, it was one of the best choices I ever made in this journey of ours called life. Not only did it give the North London Derby an extra exciting edge, it also gave way to years and years of banter, and almost being hung by the net curtain wire by my younger brother, Jae.

Remember the 5-0 battering the Goonies took in 1983? I certainly do. We were watching it together on the TV, just the two of us, and with every goal that went in he was getting more and more frustrated. Of course I laughed and whooped and punched the air at the final whistle, much to Jae's annoyance and he would have wrapped the curtain wire around my throat as I wound him up. But what a game!

For years I have had to put up a battle against my family trying to convert me into joining 'Gooniedom'. Here I am, almost 30 years later, and I am still giving as good as I get in the banter department and loving the fact that I can laugh my socks off at the league positions right now.

There have been plenty of times when I've had to take it on the chin – we all know how up and down Spurs can be. But we are deep into the 2011-12 season as I write and all is looking bright for the Lilywhites. Perhaps a dangerous thought to commit to paper.

Most of my fondest Spurs memories are, naturally, of watching the North London Derbies, and without question the best was on April 14 1991, the FA cup semi-final at Wembley. This was the match in which Gazza's spectacular free kick from 35 yards gave us an early lead.

I was was four months pregnant with my first child , but still managed to 'whoop whoop' and not wet myself at the absolute awe I felt as the ball went flying past Arsenal goalkeeper David Seaman, straight into the top corner like a rocket.

A 3-1 triumph over the Arsenal, with Gary Lineker scoring the other two goals brought the biggest smile you could ever see on the faces of Gazza and manager Terry Venables. We destroyed Arsenal's dreams of getting the double, shame that!

I didn't even know at the time that Gazza had only recently had a groin operation. That made it even more special in my eyes. What a legend. The only down side to that match was not watching it with my family. Oh, how I gloated when I did see them though, not one of them able to look me in the eye and acknowledge Gazza's genius.

I don't watch many of the matches with my family these days. They seem to think I'm 'well past' the age that banter is acceptable. All I can say is: "Pah, no way, not ever".

I did mention that 'most' of my fondest memories were the Spurs v Arsenal games (especially when Spurs have won). But my absolute favourite and cherished memory was at a Spurs road show at the British Aerospace centre in Hatfield in the mid-80s.

I can't recall the exact year. I was in my early teens, and I remember the moment well because it was crazy and funny and unforgettable all at the same time.

It was the moment I got my most treasured claim to fame by pinching Gary Mabbutt's bum! The Spurs players were playing an exhibition game of 'beat the goalie' and Gary – a true Lane Legend – just happened to bend over right in front of me.

There is little I can say in my defence other than I was a mischievous teenage girl. I instinctively reached out from the touchline and pinched my hero's bum through his tracksuit bottoms.

It was hilarious, and for my sins I was picked up by my all-time favourite player Glenn Hoddle – aided and abetted by Chris Waddle – and plonked head first in a big metal drum by the side of the makeshift pitch.

What a memory! I thought I was the luckiest girl ever to have been put in a bin by my childhood crush. My schoolgirl friends couldn't understand why I was so happy about this treatment, but how would they understand when they weren't, and still aren't, into football like I was and still am.

My love of football and Spurs meant I had a strong connection with my schoolboy friends, and they could not believe I could give as good as I got in the banter department. I didn't try to impress the boys with short skirts and makeup. Nope, a footie top, jeans and trainers were my choice of attire, and any chatting up had to include football, or I was not interested.

I was one of the boys, and to this day, still am and I love it. So I was delighted to manage what I am sure no other Spurs fan has ever done – pinch Gary Mabbutt's bum, and then have what I considered to be the honour of being dumped in a bin by my idols Glenn Hoddle and Chris Waddle.

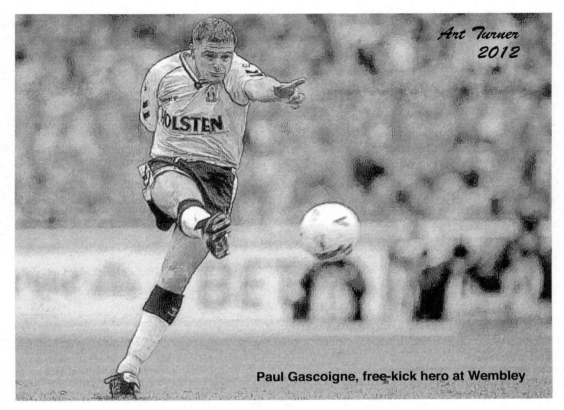

Art Turner
2012

Paul Gascoigne, free-kick hero at Wembley

After I had clambered out of the bin I stood there grinning like a Cheshire cat, until my girl friends got bored and dragged me away to the nearby fair. When I went back some hours later the Spurs road show had packed up and gone, vanished. All that remained was the bin.

The memory still makes me smile today, and despite three of my four children being 'Goonies', I still like to tell them my story. My youngest child, the one with sense, is only five so not quite old enough to understand. In a few years and with the help of Google Images, I will be repeating my claim to fame, armed with photos of my 'heroes' and tell him how that moment alone was enough to secure the fact that Spurs were my team – and it wasn't just because I felt rebellious. I will work hard at stopping him following the rest of the family down the red road.

On top of everything, I get to be a football guru for my good friend Ben – my amazing Ben – who unfortunately, for various reasons , cannot get to watch the football, and so I am his eyes and I fill him in with all the news about our great club.

Thinking back, there was always something about the cockerel that lured me, and no amount of teasing or good old banter from my family would (or will) change my mind.

I am planning a family photograph with 'that lot' in their Arsenal tops, and me and my youngest son in our Spurs strip. There will be sixteen people in the picture but it's the two in blue and white who will stand out the most.

PAUL BESTALL
Occupation: Charity Worker
Age: 39
Location: Derbyshire, via Yorkshire
Spurs fan since: 1982
All-time favourite player: Paul Gascoigne
Website: www.epltalk.com

Paul has been travelling the country following Spurs for over 20 years from his home in Derbyshire. A former lead writer for EPLtalk.com, Paul also manages up and coming Sheffield band Gypsy Toes, who tend to lead him astray!

MY love affair with Tottenham began in somewhat curious circumstances as an eight year old boy, when a covert mission saw me attend the 1981 FA Cup Final with an uncle and cousin, while my parents sat at home oblivious to my whereabouts.

Back in 1981 I'd only ever attended one football match, a first round FA Cup tie between my local team Barnsley and Worksop Town in November 1978. All I can remember from that day is the result, Barnsley winning 5-1, and the sea of Worksop Town fans decked out in orange and black striped top hats, scarves and rosettes. I recall nothing of the game, the goal scorers or the weather, just the result and the tiger-striped fans dancing in the away end.

At the time, all my family were Liverpool fans, but to be honest I wasn't really interested in football at that age. They'd got me a kit, with the number 7 on the back, as my mother's hero was Kenny Dalglish. I was more interested in Spiderman, Dracula and enjoying Bugs Bunny cartoons. If football was on, it meant I wasn't going to be watching and off I'd trot to play in the garden, ignoring the game.

Playing football had also scarred me at an early age. A busted nose aged five had put me off for life and I had announced to my mother that I didn't like a game that hurt. As the years have gone by, the physical pain has been replaced by the emotionally draining attachment I have to Spurs and what we've been through together in the 30 years since.

Yet by the beginning of the 1980-81 season, I had started playing the game more and watching it whenever I could, galvanised by the 1980 European Championships. I had been bitten by the bug and I was developing a healthy interest in the game. My parents continued to shower me with Liverpool kits and memorabilia, but it just didn't feel right. I wanted to choose my own club and I wasn't overly keen on red shirts. But back then I wasn't aware of any other teams that played football apart from the constant trio of Liverpool, Barnsley and England.

The turning point was Christmas 1980 and the visit of my cousin. As his main present, he'd received the most beautiful football kit I had ever seen, a vision of shining white and blue with a number 10 on the back. I loved it, but my parents were adamant, they were Liverpool fans and therefore, so was I. Devastated, I sulked the rest of the day but before we went to bed my cousin promised me that if this team, Tottenham Hotspur, got to the Cup Final, he'd get my Uncle Ken to take me with him. I was ecstatic. It was the best Christmas present ever, despite it being an intangible gift.

I went to sleep that night dreaming of wearing the white shirt; of watching this new team of Hotspur and hoping they'd get to the Cup Final. As the rounds went by, I nervously waited for the results to come in on Grandstand, watching the vidi-printer as it revealed a stream of magical names and places I'd never heard of or been to. But it was only Tottenham's name that I cared about.

Queen's Park Rangers were the first to fall after a replay, which I didn't understand at the time. Four months later, I was more than aware of what a replay meant! Hull City and Coventry were neatly put to the sword and little Exeter City had their big day out at White Hart Lane but went down 2-0.

My uncle and cousin travelled up for the semi-final against a scary-sounding team called Wolves, which was to be played in the next big city to where I lived at the time – at Sheffield Wednesday's Hillsborough ground. Imagine my excitement when they told me that they'd got me a ticket ,too!

Looking back, I can't believe what happened that afternoon. I was a little too young to understand the events of that day until the horrors of Hillsborough in1989 during the Liverpool-Nottingham Forest Cup semi-final. And until that day I don't know if I'd suppressed the memories of the screaming, the crush, the crying, thinking that was what being at a big game was like. I know now that I – and scores of other Tottenham fans – were lucky to escape with our lives. Yes, the crowd crush was that terrifying. Yet I remembered none of it until the nightmare events of April 15 1989. I cried for two days as everything came flooding back. My frightening experiences on the Hillsborough terraces in 1981 were – in hindsight – a sign of a tragedy waiting to happen.

The incident made such an enormous impact, I think that's when I first really fell in love with Tottenham. After the match, my uncle and cousin just sat in the car for about 30 minutes in silence. I thought they were angry because Wolves had scored an injury-time penalty to force a replay, but they were in shock because of what we had been through during the pushing, jostling and ridiculously dangerous crowd-packing.

They were trying not to show fear in front of their little cousin and nephew Paul, aged eight and half. Eventually normality was resumed and they agreed that the promise of taking me to the FA Cup Final still stood as long as Tottenham won the replay. I told them to put a bet on a 3-0 win and to put 10p on for me.

Four days later, at a ground called the Dump apparently (ok, it was Highbury), they did indeed win 3-0 and I collected £1.50 for my bet!

As the final drew nearer, my excitement was almost overwhelming. I couldn't sleep properly. I had started playing football every day, whenever and wherever I could. I wrote my Christmas list in May, asking for some new football boots, shin pads and a beautiful, shiny, pristine white Tottenham shirt. My parents, surprise, surprise, were beginning to sense I no longer shared their passion for Liverpool.

Time ticked along so slowly to the point where I was sure someone had deliberately slowed it to make it seem like four months, not four weeks. At last, on the eve of the final, my uncle and cousin arrived to pick me up and take me to their home near Beverley. I'd packed my bag three days previously and jumped in the car quick as a flash. As we left, my mum gave me a big kiss and as the car set off, told me to enjoy the zoo? Zoo, what zoo? I wasn't going to the zoo was I?

My uncle started laughing when I asked him if the Cup Final was going to be played at Chester Zoo. What were all the animals going to do? Where could they play football at a zoo? My cousin turned to me, sharing my uncle's laughter and explained that to get me out of my parent's protective reach they had been a little economical with the truth.

They had told my parents that they'd promised me a trip to the zoo, as they didn't think Tottenham would get to the final, so had agreed to keep their promises despite the match being on television.

The next 24 hours were such a whirlwind of excitement that I can scarcely picture it all clearly anymore. I remember seeing the Twin Towers for the first time, hearing the songs, wondering at the flags, banners and the roar, oh my, the roar as the teams walked out of the tunnel on to the lush green pitch.

The game seemed to last ten minutes. Band played, boring song, Manchester City scored, everyone looked fed up and then the loudest noise I had ever heard in my life exploded around me. Suddenly I was thrown up into the air. For a moment, a brief moment, I was so high above the crowd, I could see all the Tottenham players hugging, the fans jumping, the green, green pitch, everything. It was 1-1 and a Manchester City player (it was Tommy Hutchison) had scored our goal to cancel out the one he had scored for City earlier. I fell back to earth into the man's lap who was sat next to my uncle. Everyone was hugging, laughing and the noise continued. Then, suddenly it was over. The noise ended, the ground

Ossie Ardiles and Ricky Villa celebrate their 1981 triumph against Manchester City

emptied, we walked to the car and then the long drive home to Barnsley. I fell asleep and woke tucked up in my bed on Sunday morning. It was as if I had dreamt it all.

It was the moment that defined why I fell in love with Tottenham, what it meant to be a Tottenham fan, what it still means to be a Tottenham fan. Yet I never truly understood what I had been a part of until April 15 1989, and as I broke down in front of my mother, she learned all about my glorious cup run and how very close she had been to losing me. She almost lost a son, but gained a Tottenham fan and that's just the way she likes it, for all her Liverpool bias.

That little Barnsley boy danced around at home on the following Thursday as Ricky Villa's televised 'Goal of the Century' won the replay and the Cup for Tottenham.

It was much better than a visit to the zoo.

23. The Tottenham transition

SIMON GOLD
Occupation: Writer
Age: 38
Location: North London
Spurs fan since: 1981
All-time favourite player: Glenn Hoddle

Simon spent 12 years at Guinness World Records, as a writer and editor. He wrote the highly regarded *Guinness Book of Football* then moved into the TV department, working his way up to Executive Producer and travelling the world in search of the weird, wonderful and downright bizarre! He now follows a path as a creative copywriter.

MY Dad's voice was urgent and strident, agitated even.

'Come on Simon, hurry up, we're late…'

'No, I don't know where your bloody coat is…'

'Just get in the bloody car. If we can't park down Commercial Road, we'll have to walk bloody miles…'

So that was it. I found my coat and I was on my way to Spurs with my Dad for the very first time. The date was September 2 1981, and we were at home to West Ham United. We did manage to park in Commercial Road and my Dad, my Uncle Lester and I made our way towards White Hart Lane, the world-famous home of the Spurs. I had just turned eight. I was short and skinny. I was left-footed.

As we turned the corner and out on to the High Road, I was scared. There were thousands of them – of us – walking with one purpose. To go and watch Spurs play football. I have often wondered how many of them there on that day were first-timers like me and how many had been to hundreds of games, but those thoughts quickly died down and new ones came into my head.

What am I doing here? Do I even support Spurs? Just because my Dad does, does that mean I have to? Why can't I choose my own team like the other kids at school?

Like most primary schools in my part of north London in the early 80s, the Liverpool bandwagon drove past and a lot of my peers jumped on without thought, but I remember being more considerate.

Firstly, I wasn't exactly sure where Liverpool was but I knew it must have been miles away because they spoke funny and no-one round my way spoke like that, so Liverpool was out on that basis. Swansea were doing quite well, but I knew Swansea was in a whole other country so they were out, and the only other team worth considering was Arsenal, but there was a lad at school who supported the Gooners and he had a bong eye and a bit of a limp, so they were out too.

We lost 4-0. I was bored, restless and couldn't wait to get home to play Ker-Plunk. Football was rubbish.

Or was it? Was it worth giving it another chance?

The next game I went to was at home to Nottingham Forest and we went through the same nonsense getting there as we did against West Ham. But this time it was slightly different. I'd done it once and felt like a pro.

I recall a purpose to my gait. I was committed. I was joining 35,000 people who were just like me. Who liked the same thing I did. This time, I took in what was happening. I noticed the programme sellers, the guys offering roasted peanuts for 30p a bag, the touts and the wide boys all looking to make a pound note and the old turnstile guys at the entrance to the West Upper stinking of cigarettes, cheap whisky and despair.

Something happened to me that day which has never been replicated since. I was hooked. I felt funny when I saw the lush green grass and the painted white lines. I felt funny when the guy a few rows in front of us stood up just before kick-off, shouted at the top of his voice 'COME ON YOU LILYWHITES' and then sat down and never said another word. This was a ritual I was to learn he went through at every game.

We won 3-0. Micky Hazard got one and Marc Falco got two and that was it. Spurs it was. I was officially a football fan!

I went to maybe 10 or 12 games a season for the next few years until the start of the 1983-84 campaign because I shared a season ticket, but by then I was old enough to go to night games and that's when I truly fell in love. And I mean an all-encompassing love that hurt when I wasn't inside the stadium. A love that felt like a personal attack if my team was bad-mouthed in the playground, in a newspaper or on the radio. A love that knew no bounds.

These players were my heroes. I had no interest in Spiderman or computer games, I was interested in football and there was nothing that was going to get in the way.

My first night game was on September 28 1983 against Drogheda, who were apparently from Ireland somewhere. There were only 20,000 there that night but it felt like half a million. We won 8-0 with Marc Falco, Alan Brazil and Graham Roberts each getting two and Steve Archibald and Chris Hughton weighing in with one each The thrill of seeing my team play so fantastically well under an other-worldly luminescence was the most magical thing I ever saw.

On the walk home, I mentioned to my Dad that I was starving, so we dived into a little chip shop next to Seven Sisters station for the best chips I ever tasted. The evocative smell of salt and vinegar still permeates my nasal passages, as does the grease dripping down my arm and staining my sleeve, but I didn't care, this was the most amazing feeling in the world and I wanted more. Football that is, not chips.

That UEFA Cup run lives long in the memory of every Spurs fan old enough to recall it and I went to all the home legs – the 4-2 win over Feyernoord, 2-0 against Bayern Munich, 2-0 against Austria Vienna and the 1-0 win over Hadjuk Split. We were in the final against Anderlecht and I was like a kid on Christmas morning. I remember the anticipation but I knew I wouldn't be able to go.

In the last year of my primary school, all the fourth years went on a 'school journey'. A week away on Hayling Island, a tiny outpost to the right of Portsmouth and to the north-east of the Isle of Wight where we did camping, abseiling, canoeing, that sort of thing and we went the week Spurs were playing the second leg of the UEFA Cup Final. While I was looking forward to being away from home with my pals for the very first time, I was distraught I wouldn't be able to watch the game. Or so I thought.

The night of the game, our teachers let us stay up to watch it on television, but for some inexplicable reason, we were sent to bed at the end of extra-time. Why would they do such a thing? I mean, who does that? Perhaps our teachers were Arsenal fans. It was outrageous, but being 11, we did as we were told.

We all rushed back to the dorm where one thoughtful boy had a tiny transistor radio. The reception was rubbish and the volume was worse but there we were, all gathered around this matchbox-sized thing listening as intently as I can imagine all those who gathered around their wirelesses listening to Neville Chamberlain's declaration of war in September 1939. To me, the football was far more important. It was a penalty shoot-out.

Fresh from scoring an 84th minute equaliser, Graham Roberts stepped up and scored. 1-0. Next, Dane Morten Olsen had a go and missed. YESSSS! All we had to do was to keep scoring and we'd win. Marc Falco was next followed by Georges Grün, Gary Stevens, the world-class Enzo Schifo, Steve Archibald and then Franky Vercauteren. 4-3. Next, Danny Thomas walked the long, lonely walk to the penalty spot. Just pop it in Danny, that's all you have to do. Score this and the status of Lifelong Spurs Legend will be conferred unto you.

Crap. He missed. It's OK though, if they miss theirs, we win! Belgian Alexandre Czerniatynski was next. We were all as nervous as we'd ever been. Was he of the ridiculously un-Belgian name going to ruin my life?

Not a bit of it! Tony Parks pulled off a 'worldie' and we won the UEFA Cup! As a writer, one of the hardest things to do is to convey emotion and it would be remiss of me to try and re-enact quite what I felt at that precise moment. That notwithstanding, it was a feeling of pure, unadulterated joy that I don't recall experiencing before or since.

Keith Burkinshaw congratulates penalty hero Tony Parks after the UEFA Cup drama

It was the day Spurs became a living, breathing part of me, just as my arms and legs carry me physically, Spurs carry me emotionally.

The intervening 28 years have, as we know, been filled with frustration, happiness, great results and terrible results but that's what we signed up for. It's the price we pay for loving football in general and Spurs in particular. The victories are made sweeter because we went through them together and the defeats are softened because we went through them together, as one.

Spurs. Forever in my heart.

NEIL METCALFE

Occupation: Local Government
Age: 38
Location: Jarrow, Tyne & Wear
Spurs fan since: 1981
All-time favourite player: Glenn Hoddle
Website: www.neilmetcalfe.wordpress.com

Neil is Geordie born and bred but is proud to be Spurs through and through. He always gets to fixtures in the North East and the occasional trip to the Lane. Neil is a one-man army flying the Lilywhite flag on Tyneside.

HOME, for me, is Jarrow. A small shipbuilding town on the banks of the River Tyne, famous for the 1936 March and for being the birthplace of Steve Cram. Distance to White Hart Lane – 273 miles. Links to Tottenham Hotspur Football Club? None.

Well as far as I can tell there were none, not at least till Thursday May 14 1981. That, of course, is the date Ricky Villa dazzled the world, and a seven-year-old Geordie lad became a Tottenham fan. Now I can hear a few murmurs from the back and you're dead right. Yes, I am a so-called 'glory' supporter, I jumped on the bandwagon that day and have been on it ever since. May have had to push it once or twice but I'm still here!

Mind you, it very nearly wasn't that way as I actually wanted Manchester City to win in the first game and remember being gutted, really gutted, when Tommy Hutchison scored his own goal. But with my colours firmly attached to the Lilywhite mast for the replay, Ricky did his stuff and a new Spur was born.

So if that was when I became a fan, why on earth am I still one? Why didn't the fascination disappear? Why did I not go down the usual path of other Jarrovians and become a Sunderland or Newcastle fan? Quite simply, when did I fall in love with Tottenham?

Being a young supporter, and one living in the furthest, very loose boundaries of N17, my early glimpses of my new found heroes was via Match of the Day or other TV shows. My first game of any kind live and in the flesh came in October 1981, a 2-0 win at Roker Park against Sunderland. History records Micky Hazard and Steve Archibald as the scorers, but I remember very little of the game itself other than the brightness of the colours. It was a warm autumnal day, a bright blue sky overhead and I remember thinking the grass was the greenest I'd ever seen. Couple this with Sunderland's red and white stripes facing our yellow shirts (soon to be known as the '82 Cup Final kit) it all added to a kaleidoscope of colour. It was a great experience and left a lasting impression, but it certainly wasn't the moment I fell in love with the club.

My first visit to White Hart Lane didn't arrive until January 1983, again Sunderland provided the opposition. Seated in the upper tier of the East Stand I gazed out in amazement, the pristine and new West Stand staring back. Sadly those pesky Wearsiders spoiled the mood slightly by snatching a 1-1 draw. The trip though had definitely had an effect, the crush was getting serious, but it still wasn't the moment.

It finally arrived in May 1984. Now an ageing 10, I'd prepared everything. The settee was pushed round so it was practically in front of the TV, I had crisps and a drink. All that was required to complete the night was the Uefa Cup in our hands. It was time for some loving! Of course I've since found out that romance and Tottenham often walk a rocky road, and if I needed an insight into my future then this game certainly supplied it.

We'd already held Anderlecht to a 1-1 draw in Belgium and even with internationals such as Enzo Scifo and Morten Olsen against us, we were the better team (It's worth saying that I didn't truly appreciate just how good these two were until they appeared in my Mexico 86 sticker book!) The Lane was bouncing, even sat almost 300 miles away I knew that; I could feel the excitement, the anticipation. It was a typical European night in North London. We were going to win, of that there was no doubt.

Being 10 though had its problems, as did living 270 miles away. I didn't have access to local papers, to local knowledge. I'd immersed myself in all things Tottenham as much as I could but in a time well before Sky Sports, fringe players tended not to figure highly in my consciousness. I'd heard something briefly in the build up but being young I hadn't quite comprehended it all. What do you mean no Stevie Perryman? Why is Ossie only on the bench? Where's Clem, Glenn? And who the hell is Tony Parks?

To a neutral the game itself probably wasn't a classic. But, and I'm sure any Tottenham supporter will agree, to us it most certainly was! It was my first real exposure to Spurs in the all white kit and it made an impression. It was also my first real exposure to a live European night at the Lane. Prior to this all that stands out in my mind are brief highlights of the Hadjuk Split semi-final.

I remember feeling like being on a rollercoaster throughout. The now familiar churning in my stomach as attack was replaced by defence. The sickening feeling as they took the lead and a sense of desperation as the minutes ticked away. Then Ossie came on.

He'd save us, surely, trembly knees or not. And there it was, the chance. Six yards out but no, off the bar! I can't remember my exact reaction, whether it was the classic hands to the head or whether I hid behind a cushion like I was hiding from a Dr Who villain. Either way I do remember feeling devastated, and being 10 I didn't have much experience in this

Glenn Hoddle, the pass master who will always be high on the Lane Legends list

department. I didn't like it either! But all of a sudden life was joyous again. In typical Spurs fashion one minute you're down, the next you're right back up again. Graham Roberts, with a chest Desperate Dan would be proud of, barges through and it's 1-1. I'm now hyper with my mother looking on and wondering how she's going to get me to sleep. She would have the same thought and myself the same wondrous feelings in just 35 minutes time.

Penalties. Way before Turin or Wembley or Eindhoven, this was a bizarre and entirely alien concept to me and I faced it with the innocent eyes of youth and a certain amount of excitement. How on earth does this work? What will happen?

Had I known what I know now I'd have probably sported an 'oh no, not again' expression on my face. Back then I was listening to Brian Moore's commentary intently, hanging on his every word to try and follow the action. Tony saved one! That's good isn't it? Seems to be. Danny Thomas steps up. If he scores, Tottenham win, Mr Moore tells me. He doesn't, of course, and the camera focuses on his long trudge back to the centre circle, the crowd further cementing Tottenham in my heart with it's chorus of 'There's only one Danny Thomas'. I'm at a stage now where my pre-teen brain is struggling to cope with all this input and emotion. We haven't lost but likewise we haven't won. What is going on?

Then like Sly Stallone in *Escape to Victory*, Tony Parks flings himself to his right and White Hart Lane erupts. There's an eruption in Jarrow too, although with a far more squeaky and high pitched voice. We've won! The smile on my face is as wide as the Tyne. I knew they'd win but it was how they did it. Up and down throughout, at times looking so unlikely but they did it; WE did it! And I've been saying 'We' when mentioning Tottenham ever since, much to the amusement of my fellow Geordies. Because as of that night Tottenham and I were linked, a couple, a twosome.

So there you have it. The moment I fell in love with Spurs. Mind you, there is that game at St James' in 1985. Glenn Hoddle with a right footed volley, edge of the area into the top corner of the net, right in front of me. Went on to win 3-2. Magic! Yeah, it might have been that if I'm honest!

Either way I've never looked back. Why do you become a fan of a particular football club? Sometimes it's because you live there, sometimes it's because your Dad or another family member supports them and you follow in their footsteps. Sometimes it's because you see someone on the telly winning a cup. Whatever the reason you actually follow a club, you fall in love with them because you're usually young, way before you realise girls have been invented, and they do something, sometimes something small, which makes you feel unbelievable and fills you with unbridled and unadulterated joy. And that's why I love THFC. Because despite the disasters, the 7-1 drubbings, the leads thrown away in glorious comedic fashion, they always have the ability to make me feel like that 10 year old boy again.

So the number of links between Jarrow and Tottenham? It's one!

LORRETTA FONTAINE
Occupation: Careers Adviser/Project Support Officer/Writer
Age: 37
Location: North London
Spurs fan since: Early 80's
All-time favourite player: Garth Crooks

Lorretta is a fully qualified careers adviser with an insatiable appetite for creative writing. Born, raised and still living within the crowd's roar of White Hart Lane, she likes nothing better than penning thoughts about Spurs.

WHEN I was a child it was accepted that you supported your local team, not become a glory hunter follower of a club miles away. Born and raised in good old North London – Wood Green to be more precise – I was presented with two choices: The red half of North London which had a cannon, or the blue and white half of North London which had a crowing cockerel. Needless to say, the blue and white half was victorious and so the cockerel crowed its way into my life and has been an important part of it ever since. At the tender age of six, Tottenham Hotspur Football Club – the mighty Spurs – became my first true love, and thirty-two years later the love affair continues to blossom, and my love is still as strong as the day we embarked on our magical journey together.

It's not been plain sailing though. There have been tears of joy and tears of heartache along the way. But would I ever give up on my love? Absolutely never!

My early memories of Spurs players include Steve Perryman, our captain at the time, the Argentinian duo of Osvaldo Ardilles and Ricardo Villa ... "And it's still Ricky Villa" ... Apologies but whenever I hear Ricky's name, that famous quote is a must to be cried out. Then there were Steve Archibald, Glenn Hoddle, Micky Hazard, who could show our own 'Disco Benni' a thing or two about hairstyles, and, of course, my favourite Spurs player of all time, Garth Crooks.

I remember my local Londis store having a poster of Garth in their shop window. He was advertising the drink, Supermalt, in the poster. I can recollect stopping and staring at my idol in the glass window for ages, until my Mum would drag my reluctant self home. I did this for many months, until finally finding the courage to go into Londis and politely asking the shopkeeper if I could have the poster of Garth Crooks, explaining in my little voice, "I am a massive Spurs fan, Garth Crooks is my favourite player in the whole wide world and I love him very much." You can imagine my sheer joy and delight when the shopkeeper very kindly allowed me to take home the poster. I walked proudly out of the store with my hero Garth Crooks rolled up underneath my arm! He was about to be transferred for no fee to my bedroom wall.

The FA Cup has been a huge tradition at Spurs and has contributed to many a Glory, Glory occasion. I've been lucky enough to see my beloved Spurs in four FA Cup finals, and for me it is the competition which I hold most dear. As you will tell from the following memory package, it is the FA Cup that has meant most to me during my romance with Tottenham Hotspur

My memory is still warm and alive with 1981, the year that Spurs forced a replay against Manchester City after the 1-1 Tommy Hutchison/Tommy Hutchison draw at the old Twin Towers of Wembley Stadium. In the replay, which saw Steve Perryman lift the famous trophy, Ricardo Villa scored one of the greatest ever FA Cup goals

Not surprisingly, it was voted the Goal of the Century and those of us lucky enough to have seen it still talk about it with great pride as if it was scored yesterday rather than, gulp, more than 30 years ago.

It was a shining jewel of a goal that cemented Ricardo Villa's place in the hearts of the White Hart Lane faithful. What a truly Glory, Glory night that was

The following season saw Spurs book another trip down Wembley Way, this time against Queens Park Rangers. Once again the final went to a replay, and once again we saw Steve Perryman lifting the wonderful old trophy as Spurs maintained their record of never being beaten in an FA Cup final.

We then roll on to 1987, and once again Spurs found themselves at Wembley for an FA Cup final, this time against Coventry City. We were strong favourites and looking to secure a record eighth FA Cup final victory. I remember being in a ferment of excitement for weeks leading up to the final, and I had been allowed to decorate the front room window with posters of Glenn Hoddle and Chris Waddle, the golden boys at Spurs. Garth Crooks had by then been rolled up in my memory.

The final was also going to be Glenn's last game for Spurs before his move to France, which added to the importance and significance of the match.

I was jumping around with excitement and anticipation, and remember my Dad coming home from work on the Friday night before the final and heading straight back out again.

Garth Crooks, who scored 48 League goals in 125 games for Spurs

saying that he was just, "Going to see Glenn Hoddle!" Some time later he came back home armed with a load of bags from the club shop. It was filled with Spurs goodies, one of which was an FA Cup final scarf that I still proudly own today.

As I've said, when you give yourself to Spurs you have to accept it can lead to tears of joy or tears of heartache. Sadly, the 1987 FA Cup final ended in tears of heartache when we lost the final 3-2 after extra-time through a Gary Mabbutt own goal. It was a painful moment and I'll never forget locking myself in the bathroom and crying my eyes out for what seemed like an eternity after we had lost. To say that I was inconsolable is an understatement. That's true love for you. It can hurt like hell.

Roll on to 1991 and Spurs had booked themselves an FA Cup semi-final spot against none other than the old enemy from the other end of the Seven Sisters Road. I cannot bring myself to type their name, but you will know the team I mean. It was the first sem-final ever played at Wembley, which added to the magnitude of the occasion. It is glorious history how Paul Gascoigne – the one and only Gazza – scored one of the greatest goals in Spurs history to inspire a 3-1 victory over *that* team. His free-kick hit the back of the net like a rocket, and the cheers from the blue and white side of North London could be heard on the Moon.

Then the cruel side of football as we watched a tearful Gazza stretchered off in the final, with the consolation of a 2-1 victory over Brian Clough's Nottingham Forest by a Spurs team masterminded by El Tel, Terry Venables.

My love for Spurs has never flickered nor faltered through all the ups and downs of the League, but it is the FA Cup that has made the heart beat fastest, and as I close my chapter I wonder if Uncle Harry Redknapp can be the latest Spurs manager to bring the genie out of the FA Cup?

It is a love that burns as strong today as back when it first caught light 32 years ago, and it will never, ever die. Win, lose or draw I am proud of my beloved Spurs through both the good times and the bad. Tottenham Til I Die!

TOMMY MAGUIRE
Occupation: Manager, Business Process Outsourcing
Age: 37
Location: Dublin, via Belfast and North London
Spurs fan since: As long as I can remember
All-time favourite player: Glenn Hoddle
Websites: www.hotspur1882.wordpress.com
www.spursfuture.org

Tommy was born in Wood Green, 'around the corner' to White Hart Lane. He grew up in London during the Burkinshaw years before moving to Belfast. "You can take the boy out of Tottenham," he says, "but you can't take Tottenham out of the boy. I will always have Lilywhite blood."

I WAS born in Wood Green, North London, in 1974, a long, wind-assisted Pat Jennings clearance from Tottenham. We lived in a 10th floor flat in Commerce Road that had a clear line of sight to what I would come to know as my spiritual home, White Hart Lane.

By 1974, the Glory-Glory years of that double winning and European Cup Winners' Cup conquering team had become treasured memories for those lucky enough to have seen this amazing squad first hand. And for others, like me, they were simply moments encapsulated in history books and anecdotes forever reminding us all of just how incredible a footballing feat Bill Nicholson had achieved with that squad.

But the years since the Glory Glory period had not gone without its own echoes of glory. From the 1967 FA Cup final victory until the moment I arrived in the world, Spurs had celebrated a brace of League Cup victories, enjoyed UEFA cup success and subsequently UEFA Cup heartbreak in the final against Feyenoord in '74.

In short, with growing up overlooking Tottenham Hotspur FC, it was impossible not to become one with the heart beating loud and proud across the way in N17. From the day I was born, I have truly had lilywhite blood coursing through my veins.

It is hard for me to say when my first real and genuine memories of Spurs imbedded themselves in my mind. I think I remember us signing Ossie and Ricky after the 1978 World Cup, but I couldn't tell you how, why, or when. I think I remember Pat Jennings and Gerry Armstrong playing for us, but can't recall an actual game they played in (I put this one down to my Irish roots and family memories of them playing for Spurs). And I think I can remember that 1981 FA Cup Final replay goal from Villa, though I can't recall much else about the game, or the draw that led to the replay.

That is the problem with memories at a young age. The lines between what we think we were a part of and what we truly lived through become blurred. The captivating recollections of others are adopted as our own as a child because of the wondrous feelings and images they conjure, almost like the magic of fairytales and urban legend.

What I do know today is that since I was born until 1981 there wasn't really much to remember about Spurs other than some of the more notable players that proudly wore the Tottenham shirt. And probably my more vivid Spurs memories of my childhood was trading Panini stickers in the playground of St Paul's Primary School. It was there I learned the true value of a player and that Steve Perryman and Glenn Hoddle stickers where worth three or four of any other player you would care to exchange. And not even an entire Arsenal team could detach me from an Archibald or Crooks. In fact, to this day, the Arsenal pages of my Panini albums remain a blank slate.

I think my first proper recollection of a Tottenham Hotspur game was the '84 UEFA Cup final, second leg. I say this is my first as it is a day I can recall from start to finish, including that moment when Danny Thomas missed his penalty in the shoot-out after extra time. Nail biting stuff but despite the nerve-wracking finish we emerged victorious. And the days after of jubilation and celebration in the Tottenham half of North London were ones I can never forget.

That UEFA Cup win made sure I had something to brag about at school. And even if I don't remember them so vividly, the FA Cup wins in '81 and '82 that preceded that European success had also given me plenty to sing about. Tottenham Hotspur had built a reputation as cup specialists, so any shortcomings in the League were of little consequence, despite the dominance of Liverpool then. We also had some of the English League's top players at White Hart Lane back then; it was the best of times! For a 10-year-old kid, these were truly my Glory-Glory days.

But while I had really only known joy at supporting Tottenham Hotspur, I had never really experienced anything more than mildly lingering disappointment at some of our poorer First Division and League Cup displays. As someone who felt he truly loved the club and everything it stood for I had never felt heartbreak at watching Spurs.

That was until 1987.

To set the scene: Spurs went in to the 1987 FA Cup final as the big favourites against Coventry City. Clive Allen had scored an incredible 48 goals for Spurs that season and was tipped to get his half century at Wembley on Cup Final Day. Spurs also boasted a squad full of quality; Waddle, Hoddle, Clemence, Stevens, Perryman, Ardilles, Claesen, and of course Gary Mabbutt. It was a team that had what many regard today as most of the club's modern legends. We looked unbeatable!

We had also finished third in the League that season, just behind the two Merseyside clubs Everton and Liverpool, with the Blues reigning supreme, (and incidentally it was a repeat of the 1st, 2nd, and 3rd of the 1984-85 season). Anything less than an emphatic Spurs victory on Cup Final day was inconceivable.

There was something else that day that made it even more special for me. I was only 12 years old but couldn't believe I was being taken to the local pub to watch a game of football. First ever time I had been in a pub! And to see the place heaving with Spurs shirts and flags made it even more special. I was arm in arm and toe to toe with grown men singing Hot Shot Tottenham and Ossie's Dream. The atmosphere was electric. Not even the occasional spilling of drinks over the top of my ginger head and new Spurs shirt and scarf (bought especially for the occasion) by those fighting their way to and from the bar could dampen my mood. It was a true coming of age moment for me. I was no longer a boy, I felt like I was a full-grown man, despite my drinks being strictly restricted to Coca Cola. Nevertheless, an altogether euphoric feeling!

The sun shone brightly at Wembley. Butterflies ravaged my stomach every time the Lilywhite army surrounding me cheered the introduction of each of our players to the field of play. And a cheeky grin crept across my face every time a chorus of boos went out for the Coventry players that dared to line up against us.

The ref's whistle to start off proceedings was met with the biggest roar I can ever recall hearing in my life. It was almost primeval; a united cry of passion, of desire, of a belief that we, Tottenham Hotspur, were about to make history.

It wasn't long before the passion turned to ecstasy thanks to Clive Allen's 49th goal of the season after only a couple of minutes. Hugging, kissing, and cheering ensued, with me being lifted off my seat and plumped across the shoulders of two men singing with joy. We were one step closer to our dream.

It wasn't long though before the cheers swiftly turned to jeers. Coventry pulled one back to level the game up. And so began probably one of the most entertaining FA Cup games I can remember! Spurs took the upper hand again just before half time through Gary Mabbutt. Not known for his goal scoring skills but nonetheless a hero throughout the season for us, Gary gave us the belief, again, that the dream was back on.

The second half ripped along at a blazing pace with chances at either end. Then it came, possibly one of the finest diving headers (maybe goals) you will ever see in football, from Coventry's Keith Houchen.

And there it was ... All level ... 2-2 ...

And with that extra time was on its way as well as an uneasy feeling that perhaps, against all odds, today may not be our day. Extra time kicked off and after 6 minutes my world fell apart.

Gary Mabbutt, hero of the season and hero of the FA Cup less than an hour ago,

Gary Mabbutt, a hero and reluctant villain in the 1987 FA Cup final

became something of a villain, hitting the ball off his right knee and over the head of Ray Clemence into the back of his own net.

Silence ...

In that moment it seemed like we all knew that was it, the dream was over. Despite there being more than 20 minutes to play the faces of all of those said what I was afraid to think, and the faces of the Spurs players said it too. In a single moment all of our dreams came crashing around us.

The crowd around me simply stared at the TV in disbelief. Not a sound. It even seemed like someone had turned down the volume on the television. Time had stood still for a moment that felt like forever.

The silence was broken by one cry of "Come On You Spurs", which everyone else slowly picked up on. But their faces said it all, it was over.

As the game progressed and chances went begging I wanted to cry so badly. But I couldn't. I came to this place and became a man. There was no way I could leave again a boy. But as the final whistle came, and the boys from White Hart Lane made the long walk up the steps to collect their runners-up medals we all stood as one and gently applauded their efforts.

Then I noticed from the corner of my eye one guy, one of the those that had held me on his shoulders earlier, with his head resting on his mate, sobbing. And as I looked around, tears had filled the eyes of many as they watched on with such pride in our team, a team that deserved so much more than the season had allowed them.

And it wasn't until a comforting arm went around my shoulder that I realised tears were streaming down my face as well. And it was in that moment that I had truly come of age and understood what it was to love something so dearly that a moment in time, maybe so insignificant to others, can break your heart in two.

The image of that own goal, of Gary's face after it went in, and the sadness on the faces of that magnificent Spurs team as the final whistle blew haunted me for days, weeks even. Even now as I write this, nearly 25 years on, I still get a lump in my throat.

But that game is something, in many respects, that I will always feel a little grateful for. It was a game that confirmed for me that Spurs are more than just a team I support. It solidified my love for something that has been in my life since the day and hour I breathed my first lungful of air in this world.

I have many glorious memories of Spurs since '87; of FA Cup glory in '91, of League Cup joy, of Champions League qualification, of Klinsmann, of Gascoigne, of Lineker, of Bale versus Maicon, just to name a few of the things that make Spurs one of Europe's, arguably the world's, greatest ever club sides. And thanks to Harry Redknapp we can truly dare to dream again of former glories that have eluded us for so many years.

Tottenham Hotspur Football Club is my heart, my blood, my passion, my life. And this is something I truly know thanks to Gary Mabbutt's right knee on a sunny Saturday afternoon at Wembley in May 1987

27. The genius of Gascoigne

STUART WATTS

Occupation: Restaurant owner/operator
Age: 36
Location: North London
Spurs fan since: 1980s
All-time favourite player: Paul Gascoigne
Blog: www.thfc1882.com

Stuart was brought up in Surrey and moved to London at 17 seeking fame and fortune. Still waiting on both! Stuart writes about football, mainly focusing on Spurs but also writing for other websites on Italian football and the game in general.

As a kid in the 80's I always liked football. Loved it in fact. Always had a ball at my feet when I could, either at school or out in the street – remember when kids could play out in the streets without a care in the world? Of course before Sky's 'invention' of football what we saw on our TV screens was a mere drop in the ocean compared to todays' saturation coverage. So growing up in Surrey with no big club nearby, a lot of my early football enjoyment came from watching the national team. World Cups in '82 and '86 should have really told me what I was letting myself in for with regards to supporting England. Flattery to deceive and brave or unlucky failure mainly!

As far as club sides go, my Dad's a Manchester United fan. He'll be the first to tell you that I've generally always gone out of my way to go against what he wants. So I was never going to be one of the Home Counties fans of the Red Devils. Liverpool's dominance of the domestic scene in my childhood made it difficult not to admire what they achieved, and they had a lot of quality players too. They were good to watch but it never felt right to attach myself to them.

I enjoyed watching other teams too. Everton had their moments of glory and a good side for the most part. Villa had their early 80's success and have until recently always been fairly inoffensive. The larger than life Brian Clough and his footballing philosophy made it impossible to not cast affectionate glances in Forest's direction, but as with all the others there was no real bond, no emotional attachment. As our nearest League club was Crystal Palace we went to a few games there, but they weren't very good and I didn't like their ground. They were never going to be my team. One constant through this period was that I never enjoyed watching Arsenal. I never understood why until later.

In 1988, Marco van Basten scored an incredible goal in the European Championship final and my love affair with Dutch and Italian football was born. Still I struggled to truly identify my team at home, content with loving football and cheering on England. Then two other major things occurred in 1988 that would shape my life. My parents split up, ultimately to divorce a couple of years later. I went to live with my Mum and soon after she started seeing a really nice bloke who happened to come from a family of hugely dedicated Spurs fans. I'd always liked watching Spurs. The 86-87 team was a joy to watch and really should have won something. It wasn't just that season, though. Glenn Hoddle to this day remains one of the best players I've ever seen, a footballing deity. Ossie Ardiles, Ricky Villa, Tony Galvin, Clive Allen, Chris Waddle were all players I'd always watched with a sense of awe as they went about their football the right way. The Spurs way. The way I always knew football should be played. The other huge, life-shaping event of '88 was Tottenham's then record purchase of Paul Gascoigne.

Gazza arrived just at the time that I started regularly attending matches at White Hart Lane (I'd been before but this was the start of something constant) with my Mum's new fella. Genius had arrived. His swagger; his talent; his attitude; his crowd pleasing play; it all fitted with what I saw football as and always wanted from my team.

As I went to more and more games it truly felt that I was becoming part of something. Something massive. With my parents going through divorce, us moving from house to house, me heading into my teenage years, I guess I really needed to belong to something and have at least one constant in my life. It helped that my Mum's fella's family were all great and accepted us without reservation and that they were all such massive Lilywhites. Spurs dominated their households and conversations at dinners and parties we attended. I started playing 5-a-side with them every week, all of us lining up in our Spurs shirts against their mates with various other footballing allegiances. This was it, I was Spurs! Spurs for life! I think I always had been, it just needed releasing. I guess that sums up why I never liked Arsenal.

Paul Gascoigne continued to thrill at every twist and turn. Even as he stepped out onto the pitch you felt an exhilaration, that any given game could be the one where he elevated himself to the level of true great. The whole nation was growing to love the cheeky Geordie. His performances for Spurs were spell-binding, his dribbling ability has not been matched by an Englishman since and is unlikely to be. He always wanted the ball, and mostly got it and then did something magic with it. Whether it was a shoulder dipping run, a mesmeric turn or a defence splitting pass. You knew you were witnessing genius at work. Once in a lifetime type genius.

At Italia '90 the rest of the nation saw exactly what Spurs fans knew to be true. Gazza was a match winner, one moment plucked out of nowhere could turn a game. Or he could just dominate a whole game, with everything he touched turning to gold. Of course it also brought into stark reality his self-destructive tendencies, but this isn't about Gazza's dark

Paul Gascoigne, a genius of a footballer and a prince of clowns

side, plenty has been written about that before and no doubt will be in the future. This is about Gazza, the one-off footballer who's every touch of a ball was met with an expectation of brilliance. An expectation that he nearly always met. This is about Gazza, the unique footballer who made me Spurs to the core.

His crowning glory for Spurs is without a shadow of doubt the 1991 FA Cup semi-final at Wembley. The first North London Derby at this stage of the competition. It was the biggest game of my life to that point. Excitement and anticipation ran through every inch of my body. Strangely, and something that very rarely happens to this day where the other North London team are concerned, I felt very little in the way of nerves. I had a confidence about the game, a confidence that it was ours for the taking. Events of subsequent years knocked that confidence out of me like Mike Tyson knocking out opponent after opponent, but the feeling that day was that it was our day. The next time I felt so confident was the 2011-12 derby at The Lane, you know, the one where Kyle Walker smacked home a 25-yard winner.

Back to '91 and Gazza had been struggling with injury but it seemed unthinkable that he wouldn't get himself fit for this one. And true to the script, my hero was in the side. What an impact he made. He set about making Arsenal's day a miserable one in quick time, his brilliance ensuring we were 2-0 up in ten minutes. That free-kick is without doubt the best I have ever seen. Watching the game back now, Barry Davies legendary commentary is spine tingling 'Is Gascoigne gonna have a crack? He is you know. Oh I say! Brilliant! That is Schoolboys Own stuff!' It really was Schoolboys Own stuff. At 15 I would have baulked at the moniker 'schoolboy' for myself, preferring to think of myself as more of a young adult, but even so I was out in the streets the next day and on the playing fields on Monday trying to replicate Gazza's effort.

It wasn't just the free-kick though, as glorious as that was. His quick thinking – seeing the sort of thing that only a football genius can – created Gary Lineker's goal and really set us on our way. He almost ran himself into the ground in the first half hour and it was no surprise that he was substituted after an hour, by then, Gazza had ensured his place in Spurs folklore.

What came next, in the Final harks to his darker side and whilst it shouldn't be deleted from memory, it's not for this piece. This is a celebration of an instinctive, naturally talented footballing master and Spurs legend. Paul Gascoigne played football the way it should be played with an impish and imperious manner. His enthusiasm was infectious, it certainly infected me and he lifted crowds just by being there. He was a delight to watch and in my mind has never been matched since in a Spurs shirt. David Ginola was incredible and today Luka Modric and especially my current favourite Rafa van der Vaart are clearly world class but even they don't touch our Geordie genius.

Thanks to Paul Gascoigne – and there have been times in the ensuing years when thanks seem the farthest from my mind – I am Spurs. I am Tottenham til I die!

MATT OGBORN
Occupation: Editor/Journalist
Age: 35
Location: Surbiton
Spurs fan since: 1976
All-time favourite player: David Ginola
Website: www.thesportcollective.com
Blog: http://ogmosis.tumblr.com

Matt is the founder/editor of The Sport Collective, who has worked the football beat behind the microphone, on the printed page and online for Clubcall, Football365, Sports.com, Teletext, The Sportsman and ITV.

WHEN you are born into a gregarious family where half your Dad's side lives and breathes Arsenal, while the other half staunchly supports Spurs, getting the one up on bragging rights is par for the course. The lion's share of my life has seen us trail in the rear-view mirror of the Gunners' success resulting in a necessary thick skin, which makes the odd moments of triumph all the sweeter.

Looking back to my early years, I enjoyed an auspicious start to my life as a Lilywhite from the 1976 cot with the back-to-back FA Cup final victories in 1981 and 1982; however, I was much too young at five and then six to fully grasp their significance in the north London banter battle. And, so, it was not until the magical UEFA Cup run in the 1983-84 season that I began to properly understand how a team of 11 men in white shirts could produce such unbridled joy, and the more regular bouts of misery, in me.

A tiny, yet quick, right winger myself at that time, football was winning the upper hand in my affections lined up against the primitive computer games and BMX banditry of my youth. In fact, a day would not go by without a muddy garden kick about, school match or radio/TV game coming into the equation.

Back then, when orgiastic multi-channel sporting TV was just a dot on the media horizon, radio was an essential conduit for relaying games. So much so that the wonderful wireless voices of yesteryear became firm friends day or night, winter or spring. The tones of such as Peter Jones and Bryon Butler remain warm in my memory.

When Keith Burkinshaw's side parlayed their encouraging league position of fourth from the 1982-83 season into a place in the second tier of European competition the following one, there was no expectation of an easy ride. After all, this was the common sense era of one title for one place in the European Cup – a far cry from the bloated Champions League of today.

Tottenham were joined in the first round by fellow English sides Aston Villa, Nottingham Forest and Watford – the two Midlands sides still basking in the glow of three European Cup wins in four years between 1979 and 1982, while the Vicarage Road outfit could boast none other than John Barnes and Nigel Callaghan in their line-up. Not only that, continental behemoths Internazionale, Real Madrid and Bayern Munich were also looking to lift the trophy in May, such was the strength in depth of this once proud competition.

The fact that Spurs thumped Drogheda United 14-0 over the two legs to ease into the second round did not merit too much coverage in the press; nevertheless it sparked my imagination and dreams of a Lilywhite holding the trophy aloft.

The second round against Feyenoord raised the interest level all round, especially in my household as my Dad had Dutch work colleagues who were loyal Ajax fans and keen to see their rivals beaten soundly. The pre-match talk was about Glenn Hoddle taking on a veteran Johan Cruyff and we were not disappointed as Hoddle inspired us to a 4-2 win at the Lane, Chris Hughton and Tony Galvin sealing the tie in Holland.

As you can imagine, by this time, the sense of anticipation was hotting up in the Ogborn household. Giddy with Hoddle's mastery, we knew Burkinshaw's troops would need more of the same when we travelled to Bayern Munich for the first third-round leg. Needless to say, we were given a classic Spurs reality check when the Germans edged us 1-0 in Bavaria to put our hopes and dreams on hold.

With only seven and nine years on the clock respectively, my elder brother and I had not yet become accustomed to the lofty aspirations and resulting failures that have dogged the majority of the years since. As for our father, he had grown up on a healthy diet of our only two championship wins in 1951 and 1961, which were handsomely supplemented by the regular FA Cup, League Cup and UEFA Cup victories in the interim.

Thankfully for all us Spurs fans, Mark Falco capped a dream Lane comeback that the team used to fuel a routine quarter-final victory over Austria Vienna.

It was the semi-final against Hajduk Split, though, that truly captured my imagination as I prepared for my eighth birthday on April 24. The first leg had left me somewhat down on my luck, the classy Yugoslav side overturning Falco's opener to head over to north London the day after my birthday with a precious one-goal lead.

The birthday celebrations had given me a welcome kick up the backside when I tuned

Micky Hazard, a midfield maestro for Tottenham in the 1980s

in that night. Ear pressed close to the kitchen radio down in Surrey, I bounced excitedly from foot to foot as our boys zipped the ball around the pitch early doors.

I was hoping that we could nick a late goal therefore, when our impish midfielder Micky Hazard popped up in the sixth minute to level the aggregate score with a fizzing drive, I went ballistic, no two ways about it. I still had more than 80 minutes to go, however, and I near enough dug my fingernails clean into the kitchen counter urging them to hold on.

There is something extra sweet about winning on the back of a European away goal, Falco's Split net buster no doubt sowing the seed for my particular fascination with this aspect of the beautiful game. To be completely honest the nerve-jangling final victory over the bribery tainted Anderlecht side does not rank as high as that night hovering by the wireless, despite the heroics of Tony Parks, Graham Roberts and company.

The fact that I only had a vague idea where Split was added to the mystery along with the glowing reputations that the team and elegant players such as Blaz Sliskovic had ahead of the tie.

You can bet your life that I took football and Spurs even more seriously in the wake of that glorious European adventure. My intense love for the club, which will forever be in my heart, was given an extra boost when my Dad took my brother and I to see David Pleat's masterful 1986-87 side take on our nearest geographical top-flight club Wimbledon in the FA Cup sixth round at Plough Lane.

Chrissy Waddle's delightful piece of trickery to bamboozle their keeper Dave Beasant from a tight angle, dead level with my bedazzled 10-year-old eyes, and Hoddle's imperious free-kick proved the icing on my childhood Spurs cake.

I went on to have trials with the Dons a few years later, my diminutive stature leaving me – ahem – short of realising my own football ambitions. Nevertheless I have been lucky enough to commentate on and cover games from the press box at White Hart Lane and elsewhere as a sports journalist since 1994, the thrill of a swift attacking move or beautifully timed tackle taking me back to that glorious night on April 25 1984 when midfield maestro Hazard took the Micky out of those mercurial men from Split.

HUGH KLEINBERG
Occupation: Lawyer
Age: 35
Location: London
Spurs fan since: 1983
All-time favourite player: Glenn Hoddle
Website: www.coconutsandalcohol.wordpress.com

Hugh was born and raised in Scotland, from where he kept a long-range view of Tottenham until his work as a lawyer brought him to a London base and easy access to what he describes as "the magical place that is White Hart Lane."

A S the name may or may not hint, I am of good Tottenham stock. My Dad, Hackney born and bred, was a regular at the Lane in and around the Double year. But by the time I came along my parents had lived in Scotland for 10 years.

So Dad's Spurs following was restricted to listening to the radio and reading the newspaper reports. It's not just that the internet didn't exist. North of the border, *Match of the Day* didn't exist either. This was the early 1980s. A pre-internet, pre-Premiership era, and Tottenham Hotspur did not feature prominently on *Scotsport*. I have no memory of my Dad trying to indoctrinate me either. In an outbreak of responsible parenting that could so easily have had disastrous consequences, I was left to make up my own mind.

Fortunately Glasgow is fertile ground for a growing obsession with the game. From a pre-school age, something took hold. And whilst my Dad never forced me into liking football, he wasn't about to ignore potential when it began to show. Here was an opportunity to watch live sport under the guise of "spending time with his son". And so a childhood reared on Scottish football ensued.

Celtic and Rangers, of course, but plenty more. Trips to Falkirk or Fir Park. Love Street or Kilbowie. I would dance on the streets of Raith and bow to the Queen of the South. Sometimes the football was pure comedy, but to me those names still conjure up a certain romance. I knew that if I wanted to experience real drama, though, I needed to pick a team.

At the age of six my football watching world didn't stretch much further than 20 miles beyond Glasgow. The Old Firm (or one of them, anyway) was an obvious option but my sensible, football-hating mother spotted the advantages in keeping me out of that particular argument, and so a reluctant offer was made. I could have a football strip, so long as it didn't belong to one of the Glasgow giants. Aberdeen, doing so well with that nice Mr Ferguson, was suggested. How about a Scotland top? Or how about, a little throwaway and somewhat garbled, "Spurstheteamyourfathersupports?"

It was my sliding doors moment. But it was no mere dalliance with Gwyneth Paltrow at risk. It was so much more than that. It was a meaningful relationship with David Tuttle. With 3-0 home defeats to Sheffield Wednesday, but also 5-1 victories in semi-final second legs. An unhealthy obsession with loyalty points and half-time bagels.

Aiming for fourth bottom occasionally, and then aiming for fourth. Gary Lineker and Gary Doherty. David Ginola and Jason Dozzell. the splendidly loyal Ledley King and the not quite so loyal Sol Campbell.

It was a life-changing decision but by chance – or fate - the Lilywhites were in town. I don't remember much about the Celtic v Tottenham friendly at Parkhead on 16 August 1983. I just remember an overriding sense that this would be the team for me. Perhaps it was the stardust of Hoddle and Ardiles. Perhaps it was a son picking up on the obvious enthusiasm of his father – he'd never been this excited pointing out players at Airdrieonians. Perhaps I just wanted a strip, any strip. Whatever the reason, that day my fate was sealed.

I don't want to overplay how 'different' this made me from normal kids – it's not as if I got into *rugby* – but if you want to leave classmates nonplussed, telling them you support Tottenham Hotspur in 1980s Glasgow is a good way to go about it. There were no Arsenal fans to lord over or avoid after a derby. No-one ridiculed me because no-one really cared about English football. With my peers unconcerned, I could have dropped the whole thing. Instead I chose to embrace it. There's some corner of a Scottish playground that will forever be Tottenham Hotspur.

White Hart Lane was an almost mythical place. I knew it actually existed but it didn't really occur to me that I could go there. Being a Tottenham fan didn't mean going to the games. It meant forcing my dad to drive down to the border, park the car in a layby on a freezing hill and pick up a signal from England. We'd watch a live game on his (cutting edge at the time) three inch black and white portable TV and then drive back. The 1980s really was a miserable time. We were all sat around waiting for satellite television to be invented.

Eventually, at the advanced age of 12, I would go to White Hart Lane. My first game was Erik Thorstvedt's disastrous debut against Nottingham Forest. By this point the idea that I could actually live here and watch them all the time was dawning on me. I'd love to

Gary Doherty, played 64 Premier League games for Spurs after arriving from Luton

say I moved here for work, or because London is a great international city. Sometimes I do. Maybe there's some truth in that. Maybe I can't admit to myself that I've based important life decisions around Tottenham Hotspur.

In so many ways it's very hard as an adult to put yourself back in the mind-set you had as a child. But we football fans are lucky. For me it happens every time I make that walk up the High Road and see the stadium looming. I might not have spent my childhood here, but I spent my childhood dreaming about it.

Some kids discover books, or music, or clothes. It just so happened that I'd got fixated on Spurs. It may look like Tottenham to normal folk, but to me it's a magical place. And next time I moan about the walk to the ground, I'll remind myself that it's a lot easier to see my team than it would be if I'd picked Aberdeen. I'll remind myself that, short of being on the pitch, I'm living my childhood dream.

I suppose there are down sides of being a Scottish Spurs fan. An unexpected accent runs the risk of being labelled a glory fan. Please please please let that happen! Some of the songs present a challenge – I can either put on a ridiculous Cockney accent for "We are Tottenham from the Laaaane" or I can stand out like Peter Crouch hiding behind a dwarf's hat. The anti Scottish 'humour' has died down since Hutton left, though.

But I can't really see how else it could have turned out. Some things are meant to be. It was always going to be Tottenham Hotspur. It's in the blood.

AIDAN RADNEDGE

Occupation: Journalist
Age: 34
Location: Finchley, North London
Spurs fan since: 1981
All-time favourite player: Glenn Hoddle
Blog: www.aidanrad.blogspot.com

Aidan is chief reporter of *Metro* newspaper in the UK and co-author of several books about football and the Olympics. He has covered World Cups and European Championships, but his chief footballing focus has been Tottenham ever since receiving a replica shirt for his fifth birthday. His father, Keir, is a leading authority on world football.

NO one should ever forget the first Tottenham side they saw and I can feel confident mine merit their vaunted place in the club's history books.

There was skipper Stevie Perryman driving the ball forward from defence with fierce purpose yet serene assurance. Deep in midfield, appearing on the right wing or even occasionally arriving in the six-yard box himself glided Glenn Hoddle, arcing passes as languorous as they were audacious as they were precise.

Then, reaping the benefits up-front were those two deadly strikers blending emphatic finishing with quicksilver improvisation – no, not Crooks and Archibald, but Colin Lee and Ian Moores.

For this was not the early-Eighties vintage marching to glory both at home and abroad, but the inglorious late-Seventies side serving a year's exile in the Second Division.

And my "memory" of their most eye-catching display is a confection of subsequent discovery and research, rather than the impact made on the day itself. After all, I was only three months old at the time.

Faith in fate can unite football fans of any persuasion – destiny can feel like a blessing, it can feel like a curse, yet it can always feel natural.

Hindsight helps, of course, but how easy it is to reflect on the inevitability of an ex-Tottenham man scoring the winner against us.

Or how "typical Spurs" to lose 4-3 after leading 3-0 against a team down to ten men, or succumb to mass sickness when on the verge of European Cup qualification, or get bought by the world's tightest billionaire.

Then again, there are players who come to fit the club like a plus-sized Pat Jennings glove, earning tributes such as the current chant hailing Gareth Bale as "born to play for Spurs".

I don't claim to have been born to support Spurs – but was cheered to discover I was at least swift in playing catch-up.

Becoming a Spurs fan at an age too young to remember is no rare nor startling claim, I know. Many will have learnt Dad made the choice for them even before birth, perhaps even laying down a marker in the maternity ward with a blue-and-white flag or cuddly Chirpy. My cousin was barely a day old when his Wolves-supporting father had smothered his hospital bed in a huge yellow – sorry, old gold – and black rosette. Then again, he grew up to work for Aston Villa, a reminder some kids will always rebel against their parents.

My Tottenham-following infancy, however, came without my own parents' knowledge nor intention – even despite my father's obsession with the game as a football journalist.

He did actually choose Spurs for me to support – it's just he was five years late.

While he was away writing about football, my mum was often left at home alone to bring up their firstborn baby in 1977, and sweetly opted to record such momentous months in a diary.

It was only more than two decades later that, in a clear-out of my old bedroom, I found a scrapbook of my first year – stuffed with cards, hospital records and my mum's wonkily-typewritten journal. The entry that leapt out was for October 22, 1977, as she poured out her frustration at my refusal to stop bawling – before feeling wry relief at what finally silenced me.

She had switched on the television. And it was *Match Of The Day.*

Like father like son, I was quickly transfixed – and my mum was doubly amused to notice my dad's team Bristol Rovers were being trounced 9-0.

So far, so near. But, like any Spurs fan reading this, the twenty-something me instantly recognised that scoreline – and knew the away team running riot was, well, Tottenham.

It would not be until my fifth birthday that I received my first Spurs shirt, my dad having ruled them rather than Arsenal a more wholesome option for a North London-raised son.

I later heard Spurs' closest challengers for my affections – that is, via my dad – were not Arsenal but QPR, though they had just been beaten by Tottenham in that year's FA Cup final.

Ian Moores, whose goals helped Spurs bounce right back to the First Division

That second successive FA Cup meant Tottenham would have looked the ideal and obvious option, and more silverware – the UEFA Cup – would be lifted by the time I made my first White Hart Lane visit.

That trip came in 1985, after three trophies in four years. Since then, we've won three in 26. Going back to Fate, perhaps I'm the curse.

Yet I know such talk of omens is too often overblown and self-obsessed – for individuals, and for clubs, all competing for hard-luck-story status unique to none, available anywhere.

That first visit was to witness a 3-2 home defeat by Ipswich Town, despite a late brace by Spurs substitute David Leworthy.

Luckily affections towards Spurs were already fixed, otherwise the tactical line-ups on the back of the programme might have tempted me towards the side featuring so exotic a name as Romeo Zondervan.

My dad's job meant he would attend a top-flight football match every Saturday, and from that day on an occasional treat would be the chance to accompany him.

Even more of a privilege would be if he were sent to cover Spurs, but more often than not my matchday experiences would wander elsewhere – well, anywhere in or between London and the Midlands.

I remember watching Gary Lineker's league debut for Everton – a 3-1 defeat for the champions at his former club Leicester City, though I didn't notice an offside flag and thought it 3-2 until Radio 2's Final Score.

Another random journey took us to Plough Lane and Vinnie Jones' second debut for Wimbledon, inevitably ending in an early bath for him.

That match also featured one of the most spectacular fingertip saves I have ever seen, though sadly for Blackburn Rovers it was not from but by their striker Mike Newell, and he too was dismissed.

Those days tagging along with a football journalist were chiefly memorable for the view from the White Hart Lane press seats – that is, right next to the Spurs dug-out.

There I had packets of crisps raided by a leaning-over Paul Gascoigne and learnt swearwords from Chris Waddle as he ambled the touchline disputing accusations of laziness from his own bench.

I marvelled at the tireless enthusiasm of never-had-a-bad-game Paul Allen – and even more at the bravery of Gudni Bergsson, squaring up to Stuart Pearce while warming up.

I also overheard long-retired Kevin Keegan, during a Peter Shilton testimonial for some reason staged at Spurs, promising to come on as a sub and score with a diving header – before instantly, implausibly doing so.

Those childhood memories remain fresh – at the expense, no doubt, of more useful information – and retain a childlike appeal no matter what drab and dispiriting, or thrilling and enthralling, days as an adult Tottenham addict have followed.

And they came rushing back, on stumbling across that unknowingly-knowing diary, during an especially-bleak period for Spurs at the start of this century.

My club allegiance may not really have been written in the stars.

Yet at the very least I very early on knew what I liked.

Not just football. But a football club who, even in dark times – the Second Division, for goodness' sake – couldn't help but entertain.

After all, why else would *Match Of The Day* devote cameras those days to a second-tier fixture, way back before The Football League Show and when even the flagship programme beamed just three games tops?

(A Tottenham-supporting friend says that was the first match he ever attended – how cruel. He must have imagined it would always be so easy. Perhaps poor four-goal Colin Lee and hat-trick-hitting Ian Moores felt so too.)

I have to be grateful to that BBC whim, then – and also my parents, for their inadvertent influence.

Any woe my dad suffered that day could be counted his own fault.

Bristol-born and raised, he chose to support Rovers as a child, simply because his own father followed City.

Not out of petulance or pique – but because that way, they could accompany each other to a home match every single weekend.

Noble purism, speaking volumes about a love of the game itself – and perhaps an insight into a gentler, more generous era for rivalries, compared to today's bitterly spittle-flecked derbies.

But, but, but: no way shall any son (or daughter) of mine get to toddle off to "the good old Arsenal", dragging me along in return for staying politely silent every other Saturday at whatever name the Northumberland Development Project then bears.

No, I want us to unite not only in loving football, but in loving Tottenham. After all, after all the pain the club's inflicted on me, it would be unfair should s/he get to escape.

Even before we enjoy that first heart-swelling N17 adventure together, there will be the thrill of Saturday nights in watching *Match Of The Day* – and sharing those tears and/or cheers before bedtime.

Another 9-0 triumph would certainly fit the bill. That really would feel like Fate.

GLENN RUMBOL

Occupation: Telecommunications
Age: 34
Location: Stevenage
Spurs fan since: Aged 11
All-time favourite player: Paul Gascoigne

Glenn is a full time worker in the telecoms industry, and says: "I'm a father to three gorgeous kids, have a history of alcohol induced stupidity and declarations of love. I happen to have the loyal heart of a lion, but an increasing tendency to tear up at even the smallest tug on the heart strings, and this project brought me to tears ..."

WALKING through a dirty, dark train station completely surrounded by people shouting, cheering and generally sounding angry to my young ears, I remember clinging to my Dad's hand for dear life. I looked up at him to see if he was as scared as me, and was surprised to see his smiling face looking back at me. "Exciting, innit!?!" was all he said, and looked up again at the boiling sea of people all apparently heading the same way.

This is my earliest memory of being a Spurs fan. It was the 88/89 season, I was 11, and it was my first trip to "The Lane" to see Spurs play Everton. It's funny how certain things seem seared into your memory for ever, whilst other things that happen at the same time are instantly forgotten. I guess the mixture of fear and excitement of that moment were enough to ensure it was a lifelong memory, as I then don't remember the rest of the journey to the stadium. I don't even remember seeing The Lane for that first time, which is a shame, but my next vivid memory is one that all Spurs fans would undoubtedly connect with – that first time of walking out on to the terraces and being absolutely rocked by the noise of the 30,000 fans all cheering with the blue and white army. It was like someone had put earphones over my head and cranked the volume up to 11. I just stood there, staring out around the stadium, completely awestruck at the size and magnitude of The Lane. I had never in my life seen so many people in one place before, and at that point I knew it was the place for me. Suddenly, I felt like a man.

From there my memory jumps to the moment Paul Gascoigne, my boyhood hero, ran down the touchline with the ball, arm in a cast, feet seemingly moving at the speed of light, dancing this way and that like a Matador, before suddenly shifting back on to his right and swinging the ball into the box. The roar from the crowd enveloped my ears once again, but instead of fear I felt nothing but jubilation. I can only compare it to a religious zealot appearing to be touched by God for the first time. The feeling of complete and utter awe channelled to just one person, by so many. Gazza turned to our side of the stadium, and saluted with his plaster clad arm. To this day, I swear he looked at me, and me alone. Either way, I was jumping around like a disco dancer on happy pills.

I don't really remember much of the game itself, other than feeling upset when we conceded first, then feeling more positive when we equalised, then going absolutely nuts when we scored the winner. You could almost say it was the perfect "first game", as it was everything that is addictive about football in general and Tottenham in particular. Triumph over adversity, a hard fought victory, patience over promise, all those cliché's that line every red top's headlines, week-in week-out, and I lived it for those 90-minutes, and I lived it with my Dad.

I couldn't tell you from memory who scored the goals, but a Google search reveals it was Paul Walsh. I actually also saw the Spurs 3–0 Sheffield Wednesday game that same year, but the following season. I know from memory that we won 3-0, but I don't really remember too much specifically, except seeing my other schoolboy hero Gary Lineker scoring twice, and his iconic running off with two hands in the air celebration.

My fondest memory of Spurs is actually from later life, and something I would like to share here, even though it trespasses on very personal territory. My parents divorced around the same time as my early Tottenham memories, and so any time remembered with my Dad as a child is precious, including that first Spurs game. I only saw him every other weekend, and because of it we slowly drifted apart. I will not burden you with teen angst and drama here, but keeping to the context of this Spurs-spirited book I want to skip to April 15 2000 and my Dad's birthday.

I arranged to take him to see two other of our childhood heroes, Chas 'n' Dave, at the "Pleasure Rooms" on Tottenham High Road, just a short walk from the Stadium. I had tried to get tickets for the Spurs/Aston Villa game that day, as the Chas 'n' Dave gig was obviously timed to ensure everyone could go to the game afterwards, but it was sold out and so I thought I'd failed to make a day of it. Standing outside a battered wooden door that was apparently the entrance to the esteemed establishment, we were approached by Delboy from Only Fools and Horses. This fella could literally have just stepped off the set, he had the camel hair coat and trilby hat, but most importantly, was 100% a Cockney wide boy. Thankfully he stopped short of offering us the latest Chinese watches from the inside of his coat, but he may as well have. Don't get me wrong, he was a nice

Gary Lineker, who was a crisp finisher with Tottenham for three years

enough bloke, but was the very definition of a caricature. Speaking of which, cue the doormen, who when opening the door to let in the eager punters, were so wide they actually struggled to fit through the frame.

So, ten minutes later, we had managed to navigate the squelching wet floor of the dark and clearly misnamed "pleasure" rooms to a small table near the bar. Star of David banners and numerous Spurs paraphernalia adorned the hall, but all eyes were on the single drum set being lit on stage. Now, the prospect of seeing Chas 'n' Dave in the flesh might not seem like a dream day out, but I grew up in a very rural community, which I have recently discovered as being listed in the Guinness Book of Records as strongest claimant to being the oldest continuously inhabited place in Britain! So it was only the second time in my 22 years of life of seeing someone famous (Dawn French was my first, but that story is for another day).

By the time Chas, Dave and Mick emerged in a cloud of smoke on to the stage, my Dad was bouncing around like a schoolgirl at a Take That concert, giggling and cheering and generally being the happiest I'd seen him in a long time. I remember looking at him, wonderment in his eyes, and seeing myself 11 years ago, doing the same thing to him at that first Spurs game, only this time it was my gift to him. It's funny how life can do that to you some times, turn things around and upside down, and make you remember what's important again. I always say it was that day that I got my proper Dad back. We reconnect over a love of all things Tottenham, of which Chas and Dave are a huge part in our family. By the end of the show, we were all drunk as lords and ready to continue the fun, which led to my Dad doing the most illegal thing I have ever seen him do, and that was buying tickets from a tout. Now, I know many of you would have sneered at such behaviour, but it was only the once, and it was all for a good cause, namely, me and my Dad were having such a time, we didn't want it to end.

Alcohol plays a huge part in me forgetting what actually happened during the game, save for one flash of a quite superb overhead goal from Dion Dublin, and the fact we lost 2-4. It was the best time I've had watching Spurs lose though, and the reason I wanted to include it here as one of the reasons I love Tottenham.

Because of that day, it's not just a club to me, it's what helped me get my Dad back.

Due to the inherent nature of memories, my early recollections of Spurs are several different games possibly rolled into one, but they combine to create the everlasting "early years" of my falling in love with the club.

Every time my mind opens up the door marked "Spurs" and has a slow wander through the corridors, idly browsing the snapshots hanging from the walls, it is the same pictures I see every time, each one inciting the same excitement that I felt as a child, and re-enforcing the heartfelt belief that THIS is my team … I am Spurs.

ALEX HOAD
Occupation: Sports Reporter
Age: 30
Location: Kent
Spurs fan since: 1988-899
All-time favourite player: "Jurgen van der Gascola"
Twitter: @bigalode

Alex is an award-winning news reporter who wrote for local, regional and national newspapers before switching to sports journalism. He is a regular in the Park Lane Lower and on Spurs forums and is also an occasional blogger.

WHEN you're young you seem to draw influences from the strangest of places, neighbours' children, second-cousins, kids two years above you at school, postmen...

In later life you have to wonder what you ever saw in them that made you want to emulate them so badly, but I think, in the moment, you just want to absorb part of their identity, be it their style, musical taste or interests.

My cousin Michael must be a dozen years older than me, I'm not entirely sure, we're not close, I haven't seen him in years. But one Sunday afternoon, as a boy of seven, I thought he was the epitome of cool.

I remember shadowing him, watching what he did, following him like a puppy. I cringe now, but I think it's a rite of passage that we all go through, I've seen it happen (though sadly no youngster has yet realised that compared to me, The Fonz looks like John Motson.)

Anyway, evening arrived and Michael went into the dim living room and turned on the TV. He indulged me by patiently explaining he was a football fan and his team, Tottenham, were playing Liverpool in a big game.

'Who do you want to go for?' he asked, as the game kicked-off.

'Tottenham, of course,' I replied.

I couldn't tell you if we won or lost, let alone the score, but I do know a week later a pair of blue and white sweat-bands with the Cockerel logo arrived in the post for me. I wore them every day until they disintegrated! I haven't seen Michael in years, but, despite joking otherwise on pretty much a daily basis, I will always be grateful to him. His opening the door to Spurs was the best gift I ever got.

It seems fitting that the journey to my first ever Spurs game a couple of years later – the result of a prolonged campaign of pestering my reluctant Dad, a rugby man through-and-through with an aversion to the beautiful game – was the most arduous I have ever endured.

The sleepless-night-before-Christmas excitement behind me, my Dad and I left at first light on a Saturday morning in December 1990, for the hustle and bustle of a train ride to London to see Spurs play Sunderland.

I don't remember much before getting to Seven Sisters, but instead of taking the overland train to White Hart Lane as I would now, or walking 20-minutes up the High Road, my bewildered old man ended up taking us on a confusing and circuitous trek up the A10, Great Cambridge Road, miles in the wrong direction.

The thrill I got when I eventually saw a White Hart Lane road sign remains vivid, but sadly so does the length of the wintry walk down the road – no stadium there, by the way, don't be fooled by the name – before joining the throng of people swarming towards the ground. It sometimes takes a spot of adversity to make you truly appreciate how lucky you are, and that two-hour walk made what was to follow even more memorable.

I remember while queuing at the Park Lane turnstiles I encouraged my Dad to buy me the house which formed the corner of the south and east stands, however unfortunately I had to make do with a watery hot chocolate instead.

I recall racing up the stairs from the concourse two at a time, leaving my dad trailing in my wake until I reached the top and drank everything in, mouth agape.

The electricity was strong enough to shock you. The buzz of voices and laughter and expectation, the air thick with a cocktail of winter mist, cigar smoke, beer breath and the smell of fried onions.

To me it seemed all the colour had been sucked out of the surroundings and injected into the greenness of the White Hart Lane grass.

The coats and jackets were all slight variations of brown, grey and black, same for the hats and scarves and gloves. The drinks were tan or amber, just like the food, the seats, aisles and stadium-cladding, all dull colours. But that pitch...

I have been to hundreds of games since that day, visited stadiums around the world as well as galleries, zoos, museums and even botanical gardens, but I am yet to ever see a brighter, purer green in nature than the pitch on that day. It certainly seemed to suit Marco Gabbiadini, who proceeded to score a hat-trick against us.

The hundreds of games and goals I've witnessed since then have served to dim the memories of those first 90 minutes at the Lane, but some things withstand the test of time.

I remember the man next to me looked like one of the Scottish musical brothers The Proclaimers, with ginger curls, thick glasses, a pasty complexion and a thoroughly annoying habit of shouting 'Go on Marco' whenever Gabbiadini got the ball.

It didn't take me long to work out that he was a Sunderland fan, but, unlike today, he went unmolested by stewards for the entire game.

Art Turner
2012

Paul Walsh ... came on to the pitch like an extra from Baywatch

I recall Paul Gascoigne racing to take a corner to rapturous applause from the corner of the Shelf – oh yes, that legendary terrace was still there!

To my nine-year-old eyes it looked like a grown-up version of the ball-pits that you find at amusement parks, a pool of pulsing humanity with the occasional flailing arm or leg sticking out and laughter and chaos everywhere.

I remember being 3-1 down sometime in the last 20 minutes and looking at my Dad and him telling me he was sorry. It wasn't really his fault though, it wasn't him that gave the ball away in his own half.

Then I remember Paul Walsh being summoned from the bench and running onto the pitch like an extra from Baywatch, complete with flowing blond locks and surfer tan.

I also remember the Paxton Road stand erupting when he scored, I'm not sure if it was our second or the equaliser, he did get both, but I know I took great delight in jumping up and down on the Proclaimer's foot when it went in, and the absolute delight on my Dad's face at the final whistle that we hadn't lost my first game.

Not that there had ever been any doubt, but that was me hooked. There's just no coming back from that. Head over heels.

No impressionable child alive could possibly withstand such prolonged exposure to 'a proper Tottenham game' like that and not be hopelessly lost for life.

Since that day my life has been shaped by Tottenham Hotspur in more ways than the club will ever know.

On my first day at secondary school, an enormous place with more classrooms than there were pupils at my country primary school, and all alone, who was there to help me make new friends? 'Spurs' was.

They might not have known my name, where I lived or from which school I had come, but within an hour my new classmates knew I was Spurs, I went to games, Erik Thorstvedt was my hero and I had a signed Paul Gascoigne picture at home. Some of them are still friends to this day.

It was the same at University, 250 miles from home and not knowing a soul. What helped me break the ice? Spurs pyjamas, of course.

A Fresher's Week pyjama pub-crawl is a good way of meeting new people and 'the chicken badge,' as Luka might call it, ensured I had a ready-made circle with whom to watch that weekend's game.

Now I'm not sure whether I'm an eternal pessimist because I support Tottenham or rather I support Tottenham because I'm an eternal pessimist. I guess it's the ultimate 'Cockerel or the egg' debate. I am however positive that my early exposure to The Tottenham Way laid solid foundations for which I will always be grateful.

No matter how brilliantly things are going in life, my feet will always remain firmly on the floor, always aware that absolutely anything could happen at any time to spoil it.

Had I been brought up a Man United fan, I'm sure I'd be used to things going smoothly and, if something terrible were to somehow occur, my world would surely collapse around me. Thank you Spurs for making me a stronger, more rounded, person.

By the same token, no matter how bad things might appear, I will never lose hope. I know from 'exspurience' that something good could be right around the corner.

Going out of business next month? Don't worry, you might go and win the FA Cup. Booted out of the FA Cup and docked points? Fear not, a chap called Klinsmann's just pulled into the car park. Bottom of the league with your lowest ever points total? It's ok, you'll get into the Champions League next season!

Yes, Spurs have taught me more valuable life lessons than any teacher, lecturer, clergyman or police officer ever could, and I'll always love them for it.

SAM COLLINS

Occupation: Sports Reporter
Age: 29
Location: Putney Bridge
Spurs fan since: 1990
All-time favourite player: Paul Gascoigne

Sam currently covers Test cricket for ESPNcricinfo and is producing his first film, *Death of a Gentleman* on the future of Test cricket. Here, his attention is centred on the Tottenham past and the glory-glory days of Gazza

WITH fuel prices what they are today the chances are the modern me might never have ended up a Tottenham fan. As it is, the Spurs suits have ESSO to thank for the thousands of pounds I've poured into replica kits, match tickets and eventually season tickets in the 22 years since that great summer of 1990.

I say great flippantly, when I really have no recollection of whether anything else particularly great actually happened that summer. But England reached the World Cup semi-finals, and that will do for me.

Like most seven-year-olds I know the 1990-me was totally oblivious to any greater context, to anything anti-Bobby, to sweeper systems and the fact that England reached the semis via 1-1, 0-0, 1-0, 1-0, and 3-2, although I do vaguely remember Pavarotti.

All I cared about was ESSO football coins.

I was obsessed with the lesser-spotted Trevor Steven. Des Walker and Tony Dorigo made me rage (I had loads of them). Really though it was all about Gazza. Everyone wanted him, and I got him early. I still can't remember quite why, quite how or quite when it happened, but by the end of that summer my parents had filled up more times than an NHS hospital and I was apparently a Spurs fan.

I know this purely because my first real football memory, real in the sense that it was a rational decision to sit down and watch, rather than that fast forward rewind blur of childhood memories, occurred a few months later.

It was Spurs vs Everton, it was the ITV Sunday match, and I'd been bought the ITV-published programme from my local newsagent as a treat. Great days. Light research reveals that day to be November 28 1990, that 28,716 watched it live at Goodison Park, that it was a 1-1 draw, and that the Spurs scorer was the 'promising', later to become 'under-rated', David Howells.

I'm not sure what caused that few-month hiatus. Maybe conkers got in the way – I did live in the Kent countryside after all. Maybe my parents locked me in a cupboard. Who could blame them? It definitely wasn't cricket (now my profession), which had to wait until West Indies toured the following year to gain my trust and attention. But I got there, and fortunately I soon had *Gazza: The Real Me* (a VHS that I still own) to fill me in on what I'd missed. That video had everything: Danny Baker camping on Gazza's doorstep, Gazza actually sittin' in a sleazy snackbar stuffin' sickly sausage rolls, Gazza wearing fake tits (of course), and that moment where Baker had somehow snuck his way into the tunnel before the Man City game that opened the season. "I've got a feeling you're going to score today", said Baker to Gazza, or maybe it was Gazza. Whoever said it, he scored. Wow. Take that Colin Hendry and your weird red-purple kit.

Gazza was so good in that 1990-91 season that everything he touched turned to goals (suck it up cliché police.) That FA Cup run – bye bye Blackpool, arrivederci Oxford, piss off Portsmouth, nice try Notts County – was beyond scripting. Bar Blackpool, Gazza won them all single-handedly – personally overseeing my initiation into the Spurs tradition of making a very tasty meal out of the simplest of ingredients. Watching in my bedroom (complete with Spurs wallpaper) the MOTD highlights painstakingly taped by my parents removed NONE of the drama. And then Arsenal.

I think my parents still have the sofa that I was sitting on when Gazza stepped up for that free kick. It's definitely been re-covered though, because I sent a large glass of Ribena everywhere when it flew in the top corner. I can still see David Seaman tangled in the net. Should I put the Barry Davies commentary in? Yes, because everyone apart from Barry gets it wrong. Read this and tell me it doesn't hit you somewhere.

> *"Mabbutt has gone forward, with Stewart to the right, Lineker and Howells to the left. ... Is Gascoigne going to have a crack? ... He is you know. ...*
>
> *Oooooooooaaaahhhhhhhhhhh I sayyyyyyy!!!! ... BRILLIANT!!!*
>
> *(The charge, arm upraised, odd hair apparent) ... That is Schoolboy's Own stuff (Venables claps ...) I bet even he can't believe it. Is there anything left from this man to surprise us?!"*

It's reasonable to imagine Barry Davies had never heard of Raoul Moat back then.

I can't face discussing what happened to Gazza. I'm not sure I can even be bothered to talk about the final, about which my main recollections are the awesomeness of Roger Milford's mullet and the irony of the striking innocence of the felled Gary Charles.

Times columnist Simon Barnes wrote something after Cesc Fabregas had owned

Gordon Durie, who had the impossible job of trying to fill Gazza's boots

Juventus as an 18-year-old in 2006 – paraphrasing, it was about how there was no purer joy for any sport supporter than the thought of how good a player might become. With Gazza, for me, that day was that Arsenal semi-final. Reality sucks most of the time.

I haven't mentioned Lineker yet, whose video I also had (and still own) in its natty purple case, with it's terrible animated comic strip-device starring the legendary Gary Linekicker. Linekicker cruised round Barcelona, went back to Leicester to tell us how much he loved cricket, and generally stuck the ball in the back of the net. Not a sleazy snackbar in sight. He just wasn't Gazza, and neither was Gordon Durie, who was signed to help fill the void after his cup-final injury.

Durie sticks because of some commentary still lodged in my head, along the lines of "DURIEEEEEE" (not the greatest story) after he scored early that next season, but also because he was the first of what would become a yearly ritual – that anxious wait for summer signings. Every late July/August, my family would decamp to the home of my maternal grandmother in the Scottish borders – a different garden to ruin with footballs, Test match on the telly, and TRANSFERS.

God, those transfers – the *Scottish Express* and Ceefax were my life support machine, Tony Lewis and Richie Benaud the bip bips. I remember being almost physically sick when Chelsea beat us to Robert Fleck. I remember refusing to leave the house for a walk when we were reportedly on the verge of signing Phil Babb from Coventry in case any news broke. I remember Jason Dozzell. Above all, though, I remember Jurgen, coming as it did from nowhere. No speculation, no hint, just there on the back page. SPURS IN SHOCK KLINSMANN SWOOP – that was big enough even for the Scots. But a page in the paper and Ceefax weren't confirmation enough. I counted down the hours until we had to drive the hour to pick up my father from Berwick-upon-Tweed, clasping the coins I had half-inched from my mother's purse in my sweaty little hands. The moment we got to the station I was off like a Kevin Scott clearance, straight to the nearest phonebox, where I inhaled the cynically staggered news of the Spurs Premium rate hotline like a drunk in a bath of bourbon. IT WAS TRUE! I stole from my parents for that moment. I would do it again tomorrow for news like that.

Klinsmann was at the centre of the next three moments that really mattered. My first live game was Ipswich 1 Spurs 3 (Klinsmann 2, Dumitrescu). It wasn't the goals he scored, it was the cross for Dumitrescu, who dived full length to head it into the top corner. Klinsmann was over on my side of the pitch, and when the ball hit the net he just raised his arms, forever perfectly white in that beautiful 1994-95 kit. I was in the Ipswich section with my dad and brother (don't ask). Beside us, an Ipswich supporter whispered to no-one, "That Klinsmann. He's a class act." No Ipswich fan has ever been so right.

Klinsmann was also there on my first trip to White Hart Lane, when Bryan Roy, Stan Collymore and Lars Bohinen battered us 4-1 in a ground missing the South stand. If White Hart Lane made little impression then, the 0-0 draw with Liverpool later that season gripped. Maybe it was because it was an evening game and I was sat up high, but I've never seen a pitch look so perfectly green as that evening. Klinsmann missed a penalty, we drew 0-0, and I mistakenly abused Rob Jones thinking he was Neil Ruddock, but it was perfect. I was taken to both those games as a 12-year-old one-on-one by my then English teacher, who was later dismissed for improper conduct relating to foot-fetishism. In retrospect it was a staggeringly ordinary parental decision, and one for which I will always be grateful.

Seventeen years later I am on my sixth season ticket, get paid very little to comment on sport, and have somehow written 1500 words on supporting Spurs without mentioning Ronnie Rosenthal. Thanks ESSO.

CHARLIE PARRISH
Occupation: Journalist
Age: 28
Location: North London, via Orpington
Spurs fan since: 1989
All-time favourite player: Jürgen Klinsmann
Website: www.askmen.com
Blog: www.aspursblog.com

Charlie is the Editor of AskMen.com, the UK's biggest men's lifestyle website. He has also served at *Loaded, Zoo* and *Arena* magazines, writing for many others. He reflects movingly on how Spurs have not only taight him about football but also the meaning of life.

IN late July 1994, I was hot and fed up. I was an 11-year-old stuck on Scout camp in Dover. Worse, my father was a Scout leader, and one who admired Brian Clough's robust approach to eliminating potential charges of nepotism. Much like Nigel, praise and I were strangers when in our respective uniforms.

Factor in my growing anxiety towards starting secondary school in September, teasing from friends over my already fairly mediocre, now crooked, football team being favourites for relegation after receiving a 12 point ban and the fact I still couldn't master a running sodding bowline knot and you have a heady, silly cocktail of pre-teen angst.

Of course, that fairly mediocre, crooked football team was Tottenham Hotspur. Up until this point, I had followed their fortunes, but only as much as a pre-internet, pre-Sky Sports News, pre-teen without a Spurs-following family could allow. (Pathetically, I'd often attribute my Tottenham allegiance to deep-set family connections, but this wasn't the case. My Dad has developed a Lilywhite persuasion thanks to his two son's fanatical support. But Italia '90 and Paul Gascoigne were the real reasons. By rights, I should've followed the last two generations of Parrish men down the New Den.) Stuck on that baked campsite in Dover, things were changing between Tottenham and I.

My constant pre-camp, post-USA '94 scanning of Teletext and the *Daily Mail*'s sports pages had produced interesting news. Spurs were being linked with around 83% of the players at the World Cup, despite their embarrassing legal bother. Little did I know this was the start of my lifelong addiction to frantically, pathetically raiding myriad news sources for idle Spurs gossip.

Back in Dover and forced into transfer rumour cold turkey, I was drunk on the possibilities. Halfway through another epic, pointless hike through arid countryside, I cockily assured my Manchester United-supporting best friend our return to civilisation would be marked by pictures of one-named Brazilians holding Spurs scarves aloft. His laughter could have knocked me off the White Cliffs.

And so, after what felt like a Broadmoor ten stretch, we were finally free to go home. Home to our beds, Mega Drives, edible food and worlds that did not contain knots or flags. Instantly, my Dad transformed back into my supportive, funny, play-football-in-the-garden-with-me role model. I was even pleased to see the younger brother I spent my life bickering with in the back seat of our Toyota Previa when my mother came to collect us.

As I wearily clambered into the car, I spotted a *Daily Mail*. Quickly flipping to the back page, I was immediately floored. There appeared to be a picture of Tottenham chairman Alan Sugar shaking hands with a German superstar. They were on-board a yacht. The headline said Jürgen Klinsmann was now a Spurs player.

That back page changed everything. I read all I possibly could about our new striker, almost wearing out a 'Stars of Italia '90' VHS from all the rewinding to Jürgen's goals. Anxiety towards secondary school gave way to rolling daydreams about the havoc Jürgen, Teddy, Nicky, Ilie and Darren would cause Premier League defences. We got tropical fish, and naturally the biggest, most exotic one was named after my straw-haired idol. All before he'd kicked a ball.

I vividly remember that debut. Not that we were fortunate enough to go. Instead, I was in our garden, helping Dad mow a hedge and we had Five Live on the radio. I remember the sickening feeling as Colin Calderwood's instep cannoned in their equalizer. And then the elation as Jürgen put the game beyond doubt. It was the first time Dad let me stay up to watch *Match of the Day*.

The 1994/95 season remains my all-time favourite. Yes, I can scarcely believe I'm watching Tottenham these days as we scare European heavyweights and rivals arrive at White Hart Lane to grimly bore out a point. But '94/95 was when I fell in love. Pre-Jürgen, I'd loved Gazza and Gary Lineker and Teddy, but they weren't exotic. They weren't foreign.

And it's probably rose-tinted nostalgia, but for a season in which we finished seventh, played so terribly a club legend was fired as manager and were humiliated in an FA Cup semi, there were a huge amount of iconic moments. Jürgen's debut goal and follow-up heroics at home to Everton. Gica Popescu's coolly dispatched drive in the North London Derby. Teddy's hat-trick in a 4-2 win over an incredibly fun Newcastle team. And Jürgen's

Jürgen Klinsmann
Art Turner
2012

last minute winner at Anfield in the Cup quarter-final that would become his first tenure's purest achievement. He left the field nearly in tears that day.

I saw almost all of those moments live, with my Dad. Almost right at the beginning of the 1995/96 season, my parents separated and Dad would later disclose he'd taken me to so many games in that Jürgen season because he knew what was headed our way. In six months, I experienced glimpses of the two different styles of grief I believe we go through. First, the inconsequential, slightly embarrassing sadness that strikes us down before we're able to file things in their correct context.

Some might remember their tears at Take That splitting up. Mine was that press conference at the Comedy Store as Jürgen quietly announced he had to return home to Bayern Munich. I ran to my room and wept, all the while not knowing quite how silly it all was. And then, when Dad also left, I realised. That 1994/95 season would gain added importance with each passing year.

Because I'm a bit self-indulgent, it became easy to link Jürgen and my Dad. Going to White Hart Lane so frequently with Dad that year – often just the two of us – gave us a closeness we hadn't had before. And then, like that, it disappeared and would take nearly a decade to return. We wouldn't go to White Hart Lane together for nearly five years. Jürgen's arrival in 1994 also helped spark my love affair with Spurs. He teased me with moments of unique happiness and then exited my life before it became something tangible.

When my parents entered into their protracted and damaging break-up during that first post-Jürgen season (with poor Chris Armstrong cast as the step-Jürgen), I received a sobering, necessary reminder that life isn't always football superstars signing for your team on a yacht in Monte Carlo or idyllic Saturday afternoons spent with your Dad.

Sometimes, it's home defeats to Arsenal and genuine, awful strife affecting the ones you love. But I had also learned to appreciate those unique moments of happiness, too.

Life as a Spurs fan is about surviving the strife to enjoy those moments of unbridled, unexpected and melodramatic joy. We don't really do that gentle hum of sustained, passable success. It's what that Jürgen-inspired 1994/95 season taught me about Spurs. And it's what that Dad-inspired 1994/95 season taught me about life.

TIM FRAMP

Occupation: Independent Financial Adviser
Age: 27
Location: Guildford, Surrey
Spurs fan since: 1991
All-time favourite player: Teddy Sheringham

Tim is a Tottenham fan of more than 20 years, inspired by the great FA Cup winning team of 1991. He was a founding member of the 'We Are N17' group of Spurs supporters, who successfully campaigned against the club's proposed move to the Stratford Olympic stadium.

I WAS seven when Spurs first entered my life. The 1990 World Cup had been staged the season before and England had a couple of star players, both of whom happened to ply their trade at one Tottenham Hotspur FC. Gazza was undoubtedly, as a result of Italia '90, the biggest name in world football; a mercurial talent who doubtless needs no introduction to even the most 'armchair' of football fans. Gary Lineker, the goal poacher *extraordinaire*, had achieved similar fame, with his career taking in a stop at Barcelona before he arrived at White Hart Lane.

Like any child beginning to take an interest in football, my heroes were predictably the star players. Yet, at this stage my early interest had not yet developed into a preference when it came to club football.

It's easy to forget – particularly for those of us in our mid to late 20s – that watching football was not always as it is now. Not only did Sky not screen television matches before the 1991-92 season, the Premier League didn't exist and Sky's subscriber base was counted in their thousands, rather than millions. Indeed there is something of symmetry now, as my time as football supporter coincides neatly with the Sky/Premier League era, meaning every stat and fact that Sky wheel out tends to relate to the exact period I have been watching football.

Although my Dad is not a keen football fan (having taken the well-trodden path towards Manchester United despite having been born and raised in Surrey), he would watch matches on TV when they were being televised, as a game on TV was much more of a treat and an event than today.

For my part, I would stroll (I say stroll, people under the age of 10 rarely stroll, they dash, dart and sometimes spin, cartwheel or skip) into the living-room and I would ask my Dad, "Who's playing in red?", "Who's playing in blue?" – with the reply usually being Manchester United, Arsenal or one of the many other names with which we are all familiar. However, one day, the answer to the fateful question, "Who are the ones playing in white?" came the reply, "Tottenham Hotspur". In that instant something clicked, I don't know what, as much as anything because 20 years have passed since then, but I instantly knew there was something a bit special about that name: *Tottenham Hotspur.*

All that begs the question, what's in a name? Everything, and nothing all at once. Shakespeare's observation 'a rose by any other name would still smell as sweet' is ringing in my ears as I search for the words to describe exactly what the name Tottenham Hotspur means to me, but on this occasion it seems entirely inaccurate. Yes, of course had that collective of schoolboy cricketers formed a club in 1882 and called it Enfield Athletic or Haringey Town, there might still have been the same club built by the same group of people. The early history might still have been the same, but I can't help thinking that there are others who, like me, were attached, or even in love with that name before they ever really new anything about Tottenham Hotspur, and that some of those romantic types might never have been drawn to the club without it.

So by now we've reached 1990-91, my footballing heroes are Gazza and Lineker and conveniently my childish mind has formed an attachment with Tottenham Hotspur thanks to nothing more complicated than a romantic name. Whether it's because they happened to play for the ones in white or because they genuinely were the only names I was interested in I can't really remember, but I learned that my favourite players, indeed probably the only players I knew the names of, played for Tottenham Hotspur and with that, the deal was done.

That's how the story should go, anyway; with tales of Gazza vs Arsenal and everyone but vs Nottingham Forest in the FA Cup filling the rest of my falling-in-love-with-Tottenham tale.

Unfortunately – while I feel I remember those games like they were yesterday – I'd be lying to you and worse, to myself if I was to try and cite those games as my first true Spurs supporting memories. I am pretty sure I watched them live and even surer still that I was supporting Spurs, but as I mentioned, football wasn't big in my household and despite the fact my Manchester United-supporting father didn't make any effort to influence me, this was the early '90s, a time when every child, almost without exception, supported Manchester United. Spurs winning the FA Cup is something I look back at and watch now with a great deal of nostalgia but at the time I just didn't 'get it' like I do now.

Manager Ossie Ardiles welcomes Ilie Dumitrescu to White Hart Lane

My interest in football had taken a backseat to more important things, such as running around like a lunatic, cycling around like a lunatic and Teenage Mutant Hero Turtles. Whilst I don't remember this, I am reliably informed that there was a spell, briefly, when I believed myself to be a supporter of Manchester United. I was young, confused and dazzled by bigger boys who tricked me into thinking that supporting a football team was all about supporting the club that wins everything.

But without prompting, I somehow managed to steer clear of that obvious pitfall; again I don't remember how, but I'd found a new hero in Teddy Sheringham. I went off to the Saints Soccer School in my Spurs kit and I felt on top of the world when I got the certificate for most improved player, listing my name as "Tim 'Teddy' Framp". Yes, I got the 'he's rubbish but at least he tried' certificate, but we can gloss over that and take away from it that they compared me to a genuine Spurs great.

Finally, there is one more memory. My first real memory of a Spurs match.

This isn't the one that sealed the deal, at least not for me. I was already one of those fans who checked Teletext on a daily (hourly) basis to see whether there was a snippet of Spurs news to keep me sated and who saw that little 'Clubcall' advert telling me about a '£15M MEGA DEAL' leaving me desperate to find out. I certainly remember reading about the signing of Jürgen Klinsmann through the very same medium shortly after the signing of Illie Dumitrescu, another star of the '94 World Cup, was announced. That season was one of the rare bright spots of a very drab decade for Spurs and there are two matches from that season which I remember particularly vividly.

Both took place in the FA Cup and both were against clubs from Merseyside. Liverpool themselves were a good side at the time, consistently finishing in the upper echelons of the league and in the quarter-final of the FA Cup, at home against Spurs, were the favourites to walk away with the spoils. I don't need to tell you that the difference on that day was our German talisman.

Following that we were drawn against Everton, and this time we were the favourites. Indeed as far as the media were concerned Tottenham's name was already on the Cup, and with Klinsmann in our side the result was a foregone conclusion. The press were already talking up a dream final against Manchester United and with youthful naïvety I believed them.

I watched the game at my Aunt and Uncle's house, refusing to miss it on any account. Once again, I don't need to go into too much detail here, but it was not Klinsmann who decided the game, but Daniel Amokachi, who scored two brilliant goals to give the Toffeemen a 4-1 victory. Evertonian folklore suggests that Amokachi wasn't even supposed to be on the pitch, effectively bringing himself on while everyone was distracted with Paul Rideout's injury.

Whatever the circumstances, the heart of a young 11 year old was broken and as a result, one of my first proper memories of Spurs involves me bawling my eyes out, surrounded by my entire family, having watched my team be unceremoniously dumped out of a competition I had expected to see them win. It was no consolation to my young heart that we lost to the eventual winners and it was all capped in the heartbreaking sight of seeing my idol walk out of the club after just one – very special – year.

It was a harsh lesson in being a Spurs fan and a precursor to many a swashbuckling defeat. But to be honest, I wouldn't have it any other way, because the swashbuckling glory days I will see someday will be all the more special. Then I will be prepared to shed tears of joy.

JAMIE DUNN

Occupation: Football Writer/Website manager
Age: 26
Location: Stevenage, Herts
Spurs fan since: 1991
All-time favourite player: Jürgen Klinsmann/Ledley King
Website: www.goal.com
Blog: www.boysfromthelane.com

Jamie is a Premier League accredited football writer and site manager for Goal.com UK. He also contributes to the Spurs blog 'The Boys From White Hart Lane'. Spurs legend Ossie Ardiles has been among his favourite interviewing assignments..

I WAS NOT born to be a Tottenham fan, as my parents only took a passing interest in football. Had they been avid followers of the game it might have panned out differently for me, because my father was born and bred in the decidedly red-blooded Arsenal territory of Archway. You cannot get more Gooner than that.

Yet by the time I was six years old I was supporting Spurs. Not that I knew exactly what that meant. My next-door neighbours, who had a boy slightly older than me, were Tottenham fans, as were all my new school friends it seemed, and in 1991 Paul Gascoigne led the club to FA Cup glory with a series of sumptuous performances. And so, despite my older brother having already declared his allegiance to Liverpool, I supported Spurs.

But my love affair with Spurs doesn't begin with memories of Gazza beating David Seaman with a thunderous free kick from all of 30 yards in the FA Cup semi-final, or Barry Davies' excited commentary ("Is Gascoigne going to have a crack? He is you know…Oh I say!"), or even with tears over the mercurial Geordie's subsequent self-inflicted knee injury in the final.

In fact, it wasn't until the summer of 1994 that I really understood football, which, fortunately for me was a World Cup year. Watching USA '94 highlights on Eurosport first thing in the morning, I got my footballing education.

England, of course, failed to qualify for USA '94, which with hindsight I have always been thankful for, as I watched the tournament with no sense of patriotism and was able to enjoy the host of brilliant players on display. Bulgaria had Hristo Stoichkov. Romania

Gheorghe Hagi. Brazil Romario. Italy Roberto Baggio.

Germany had a player called Jürgen Klinsmann.

It was a disappointing World Cup for Germany by their high standards, crashing out to Bulgaria at the quarter-final stage. But Klinsmann scored five times in the tournament, the pick of the bunch a volley he teed up for himself against South Korea, one of his two goals in that game.

Klinsmann had captured my imagination, and so I was overjoyed to learn that, following the tournament, my club, Tottenham Hotspur, had managed to sign the striker from Monaco for £2m. In my youthful innocence, I had little idea of the connotations of being a German in England, nor was I aware of Klinsmann's part in England's undoing in the 1990 World Cup semi-final, or his reputation as a diver. All I knew was Tottenham had signed a football megastar, and I was excited.

Sure enough, on the opening day of the season, our summer capture proved I had just cause to have been eagerly anticipating his debut. Spurs travelled to Hillsborough to face Sheffield Wednesday on August 20, 1994 with club legend Ossie Ardiles in charge, and eager to display his array of attacking talent; Darren Anderton, Nick Barmby, and Romanian summer recruit Ilie Dumitrescu would all feature, with Teddy Sheringham partnering Klinsmann in what would be known as 'The Famous Five'. If I wasn't aware of the historical Tottenham philosophy before then, I was about to receive something of an education.

It took Spurs just 18 minutes to open the scoring, as Anderton crossed for Sheringham, who pushed the ball out from under his feet and stabbed it into the bottom corner from just inside Kevin Pressman's penalty area. The pair would combine for the second goal on the half-hour mark, as Klinsmann fed Anderton, who exchanged a neat one-two with Sheringham before making it 2-0.

After the interval though, Spurs allowed Sheffield Wednesday back into the game as Dan Petrescu slotted past Ian Walker from close range, before Colin Calderwood found the top corner of his own net to level the scores with 25 minutes to go.

But Spurs kept coming. Sheringham flicked a clearance into the path of Barmby, who drove into the penalty area and powered the ball beyond Pressman's outstretched fingertips to put Ardiles' men back in front, before Klinsmann put the game out of reach.

With the contest approaching its climax, Anderton drilled a cross into the penalty area, where a waiting Klinsmann showed expert movement to pull away from Des Walker, before hanging in mid-air and stooping to power a header past the despairing Pressman. In a nod to those critical of his theatrical exploits, the German wheeled away, before leaping to the floor and skidding on his chest along the Hillsborough turf, joined by his new Spurs team-mates.

Jurgen Klinsmann, the Spurs saviour with four goals against Wimbledon

Art Turner 2012

Just five days later, Klinsmann was at it again. Fresh off the back of what was eventually a 4-3 away win on opening day, Spurs were victors in the first home game of the season against Everton, with Klinsmann scoring both of the goals in a 2-1 triumph.

Midway through the first half, Anderton – who is at least a footnote in most of my favourite Tottenham goals and moments – delivered a corner which would eventually be guided into the path of Klinsmann by Stuart Nethercott. The striker shifted his body weight to his left foot, and watching the ball, launched his body into the air, and struck in a scissor motion past Neville Southall. It was a goal I would try to replicate in the school field and on the green near my house, much to the chagrin of my mother, who had to clean my uniform, though I never mastered it and have been unable to replicate it since.

Klinsmann's second was decidedly less complicated fare, as he nodded in from close range with Spurs holding on for a win after Paul Rideout's second half goal. But those first three strikes typified the man; instinctive, athletic, intelligent, predatory and clinical, Klinsmann could do it all, and he would go on to repeat those exploits of the opening week of the season time and again during the 1994-95 campaign.

Klinsmann scored 29 goals in all competitions, but while it was a successful period for the striker, Spurs would end the season empty handed. Ardiles was sacked as the club flirted with the lower regions of the Premier League and was replaced by Gerry Francis, who guided Tottenham to a seventh-place finish – just short of Uefa Cup qualification – and a 4-1 FA Cup semi-final defeat at the hands of Everton.

And just like that, Klinsmann was gone. I was crestfallen; unable to comprehend why my favourite player should want to depart my beloved Spurs for a return to Bayern Munich. There was some sort of altercation with chairman Alan Sugar, but football politics was not for my young mind. I was interested only in what happened on the pitch.

Of course, with hindsight, it is not so difficult to understand what was going on but I still wonder what might have been for Tottenham in 1996, had there been Klinsmann rather than Chris Armstrong.

But that was not the last we would see of Klinsmann, as our hero mended bridges with Sugar and returned for a brief loan spell to save us from relegation during the 1997-98 season. Fittingly, it was the German's four goals in a 6-2 victory that secured our Premier League status in the penultimate game of the campaign against Wimbledon. Any lingering feelings of antipathy towards Klinsmann over his previous departure among the Spurs faithful must surely have been eradicated on that day at Selhurst Park, as were any doubts over his deserved legendary status.

Over 15 years after his arrival, I still use Klinsmann as a yardstick with which to measure the quality of Tottenham strikers. None have quite met his impeccable standards during that time. Quite simply, Klinsmann was *wunderbar*.

37. Keeping it in the family

NEIL HAWKINS
Occupation: Journalism student
Age: 24
Location: Falmouth/Brighton
Spurs fan since: A day old
All-time favourite player: Jürgen Klinsmann

Neil is a young writer just starting out on his journalistic adventure. He likes nothing more than three points on a Saturday and a trophy come May. He's still waiting for that trophy though, but is eternally optimistic.

I WAS never going to have a choice as a child when it came to which club I was going to follow. I couldn't choose which club I was going to fall in and out of love with over and over again. I didn't have a say in the matter as to what team would give me stratospheric highs and plunging lows. The decision had been made many, many years ago.

My Great Granddad was there at Stamford Bridge in 1921 when Spurs beat Wolverhampton Wanderers to win the FA Cup for the second time. My Granddad was at Wembley in 1961 when Leicester City were downed 2-0 and the famous double was completed. Then my Dad was there in 1981 when Ricky Villa scored the greatest ever FA Cup final goal. So there I was, a day old, wrapped up in a brand new Hummel Spurs shirt, not knowing what glories and what traumas where being placed on my shoulders. Like I said, choice wasn't even an issue.

My first Spurs 'experience' was at three years of age being on my Dad's shoulders on Tottenham High Road, waving the cup winners flag my Grandad had just bought me. Gary Mabbutt was at the front of a bus holding the FA Cup we'd won the day previous against Nottingham Forest. Of course, I didn't know who Gary Mabbutt was, what he was holding in his hands, or the actual importance of the occasion. I had a flag, everyone was smiling and there was a lot of singing. I just didn't know how to take it all in.

Fast forward three years and the arrival of my first football love. By now I knew the way it was going to be. Saturday afternoons, 4.45pm, turn on the TV with Dad and Granddad and wait for the 'FT' to flash up on the vidi-printer. It was either a "Come on you Spurs" or "here we go again". If my memory serves correct, it was definitely more of the latter! My reaction was a pure copycat of one of my two elders. If they were happy, I was. If they were down about the result, so was I. But a strange sounding name kept on coming up in their conversation. Their faces beamed when they said his name. They could not stop salivating over a man they called Jürgen Klinsmann ...

"Right Neil, what you need to understand is this guy is good. Very good in fact. One of the best strikers in the world right now. How and why he's playing for us, we don't know, but just watch him."

So I did watch. And I kept on watching. I watched so much I knew I was falling for this game, for this player and for this club. Every week he was scoring goals. Thirty of them in that one glorious season. I still couldn't understand who this guy was, or that he was a World Cup winner. But he got me.

Of all the great things he did in a Spurs shirt, my one abiding memory is of a disallowed goal he scored at The Lane against Manchester United. The game was lost (as per usual) 1-0, but I remember him scoring and then running to the corner flag and sliding on his knees in celebration with sheer jubilation etched all over his face. Of course, he didn't realise he'd been blown offside. But that celebration! I'd never seen someone so happy to score a goal. It sticks with me because two weeks later, I played my very first game of proper football for my school. We drew 3-3. I scored, and my celebration was to run to the corner flag and replicate my very first Tottenham hero.

True love was confirmed on Saturday March 2 1996, the very first time I went through those wonderful turnstiles at that awe-inspiring Tottenham stadium. Jumping on the 243 at Wood Green with my Dad and his two Spurs-mad best mates, the bus was full of scarves and shirts, and language I would later in life find out to be known as banter! We got off the bus and walked through Bruce Castle Park, my excitement just kept on growing. The buzz was getting louder and louder. Then suddenly, I was on the High Road, and there it was, White Hart Lane. We bought a programme then went in the club shop. There was Spurs memorabilia everywhere! I didn't know where to look; I was loving it and hadn't even stepped inside the stadium yet. I was then given the tour around the ground; I had to get the 'feel for it' according to my Dad. Up the Park Lane, past the burger stalls, skipping over and around the horse muck. Turn left and down Worcester Avenue and seeing the East Stand in all its old-time glory. Turnstiles clicking and everyone wearing that pre-game 'what's going to happen today' look on their faces. Turn left again and down Paxton Road, dodging more horse muck and going against the flow of traffic of people walking towards their turnstile. Turn left once more, and back onto the High Road. I've got a feel for it now all right – get me in that stadium!

Then before I knew it, I was in. West Stand lower, in the Park Lane corner. Seeing the pitch for the first time was one of the biggest rushes I've ever had. The lush, flat and ever

Jurgen Klinsmann, a high-flying success in two spells with Spurs

so beautifully green surface was the exact surface I'd been seeing on the TV every other weekend for the past few years. Now I was here; here amongst 30,000 Spurs fans, going to church on a Saturday. I was about to witness Tottenham Hotspur for the first time. The thrills and spills. The cheers and jeers. The colour and the excitement. From memory, the game wasn't much, we beat Southampton 1-0 and Jason Dozzell scored midway through the second half. It was all over in a flash. But every second of it was pure ecstasy. Even Chris Armstrong put in a decent shift!

Since then it's been a rollercoaster, and it always will be with Spurs. It's how we like to do it. But doesn't that make it more fun? Never knowing which Spurs will show up? It was a steady and drawn out process for me to really discover and feel for this club, albeit an inevitable one. But that's what makes Spurs really special to me. It's in my blood. What I now need is my own little bit of 'I was there' cup final history. That would complete a rather nice and quite unique set. Until then, we shall just have to let the highs and lows continue. We wouldn't want it any other way now, would we?

MARK TILLEY

Occupation: Writer/Editor
Age: 23
Location: London
Spurs fan since: 1988
All-time favourite player: Dimitar Berbatov
Website: www.boysfromthelane.com

Mark is a London-based writer and the creator of Tottenham website 'The Boys From White Hart Lane'. A Spurs fan since birth, he was raised on the infuriatingly mediocre teams of the late nineties and sees the current progress of the side as a reward for his endurance.

IT was John Cleese who said, in the film *Clockwise*: "I can cope with despair but it's the hope that kills me." In all my years of supporting the great Tottenham Hotspur, I've yet to find a sentence that better summarises my devotion to the club. I am a Spurs fan as a result of parental guidance, not personal choice. There was never a decision to make. From as early as I can remember, Spurs was my life and that was that. The earliest football memories swirling around in my head consist of the old man wincing in agony as he checked Ceefax every two minutes to see if we'd conceded yet. This was staple Saturday afternoon behaviour and, before we had realised, myself and my older brother joined him in the regular weekend suffering session.

My formative Lilywhite years came in the mid to late nineties. I was alive when the likes of Waddle, Gascoigne, Lineker and Klinsmann were parading their talents at the Lane, but being too young to even comprehend what football was at the time, I never had the chance to enjoy their spells at the club. No, I was parachuted into the Spurs family during a period when mediocrity reigned supreme. My early Spurs heroes were Darren Anderton, Teddy Sheringham and Steffen Iversen – good players all – but to any fan who is currently being raised on the delights of Gareth Bale, Luka Modric and Rafael van der Vaart, be sure to count yourself extremely fortunate.

And so it was that I became increasingly comfortable with the element of despair. I'd seen us lose countless North London Derbies. We hadn't beaten Chelsea in a generation. A top half finish was generally considered to be a successful season. In short, we were in limbo. Not good enough to make an impression at the top. Not so bad that we often found ourselves in relegation dogfights.

In 1999, we found ourselves under the control of dour former Arsenal boss George Graham. His appointment as coach was not universally celebrated within the Spurs community. His ties to the enemy were allied with a reputation for producing dull, flavourless football, something that didn't sit too well with the fans who had been raised on the flair teams of years gone by. But, despite the naysayers, Graham stabilised the club after a calamitous start to the season. Spurs were noticeably more organised and, though they were unlikely to threaten Manchester United's monopoly on the domestic game, they were in comparatively healthy shape.

League progress was steady, but if there's one thing to really get the fans fired up and on side, it was a cup run. And Graham had managed to guide Spurs past the likes of Liverpool and Man Utd to the Worthington Cup final, where they would face Leicester City. It was a competition that was just starting to be treated with the contempt it is in the modern age. The Man United side we faced in the quarter final at White Hart Lane was taxing at best and a David Ginola-inspired performance put them to the sword – the Worthington Cup was the only trophy they didn't win that season.

After Wimbledon's dogged semi final challenge had been seen off over two legs, Spurs were on their way to Wembley for the first time since the 1991 FA Cup final. After spending the whole decade desperately searching for something to cheer about, here was our opportunity. I couldn't remember a more exciting day as a Spurs fan. I was 10 years old and hadn't had a moment of genuine celebration to speak of in my brief time as an ardent Lilywhite. And being the only Tottenham fan in a school full of glory-hunting Man United fans and typically smug Chelsea and Arsenal types, I was desperate for something to crow over.

The match itself was a drab affair. Unable to procure tickets, my Dad, brother and I were forced to listen to the game from the relative comfort of our south London home and what we heard was a tale of two sides effectively cancelling each other out. Leicester, guided by the respected Martin O'Neill, stuck to their task of denying Tottenham space and nullifying the threat of Ginola.

It was also a tempestuous affair – the utterly reprehensible actions of Leicester's Robbie Savage managed to sufficiently wind up the Spurs players to the point in the 60th minute of the game's first major talking point: Savage launched himself into the Spurs left back Justin Edinburgh, who immediately lashed out and raised his arms towards his assailant.

As befitting a player with such a lack of class, Savage first turned to confront Edinburgh with an entirely fake aggressive stance before turning away, clutching his face as if he'd been hit by a cannon and falling to the ground. Players from both sides surrounded the scene, Savage was booked for the initial tackle and Edinburgh was sent off. A deserved red? Perhaps, in the sense that he should never have reacted to the bait being offered to him. But it was obvious Savage's dishonest theatrics had counted against him.

The incident had a galvanising effect on the Spurs players. In the final thirty minutes of the match, it was they who looked the more likely goalscorers. It was they who started to pass the ball with more urgency and move around the field with great purpose. I sat at home, huddled against the wall and clutching to the radio in helpless anguish. The despair of losing would be fine. It was the hope that was killing me. Here we were, minutes to go in the cup final and we hadn't lost yet. We weren't 3-0 down and out of sight. We still had a shot. The dream I had of walking back into school the following Monday and proudly showing off my mock League Cup winners medal, like I'd played my own part in the game, was still alive.

The ninety minutes were up. Injury time and penalties beckoned. Not penalties, I prayed. For I had witnessed England's pain at Euro 96 and the World Cup in 1998. I knew of penalty shootout despair like all others up and down the country. Suddenly, there was excitement in the voice of the commentator. Iversen had broken down the right flank and was taking on his man. My senses heightened. My anxiety grew even more intense. Iversen won his race and fired across towards goal. It was nothing more than a hopeful shot disguised as a cross but it forced Kasey Keller, the Leicester and future Spurs 'keeper, to dive and palm the ball out with his right hand. And there was Allan Nielsen, the Danish midfielder who wasn't even a regular starter and who was the last person any Spurs fan expected would be the match decider. His full length dive allowed him to nod the ball into the back of the net and that was it. There would be no time for a Leicester comeback. The game was won.

It's difficult to put into words just how you feel when you realise your team has won a trophy for the first time in your existence. Elation is obviously a prevalent emotion but there were also elements of disbelief and shock. Looking back now, it seems silly to have become so emotionally connected to the winning of the League Cup, but at the time it seemed like the only appropriate thing to do. My entire family erupted into a state of euphoria.

Players that we had spent years deriding were suddenly immortal legends. Ramon Vega, the hapless Swiss centre back, was put on perhaps the highest pedestal he would ever sit on in his career. For a brief few hours, the eleven Spurs players that took part in that game were my lifelong idols. I believed that the win meant just as much to them as it did to me and that all of us were equals – all bonded together by the Spurs cause. This was the beginning of a new era. We were on our way to becoming a force in English football again.

Of course, we weren't. Graham lasted only another year or so before he was replaced as coach by Glenn Hoddle, at the start of yet another false dawn. Campbell vocally committed himself to staying at Spurs before refusing to sign a new contract and leaving to join Arsenal, of all teams, on a free transfer. Nielsen was again cast to the sidelines upon Tim Sherwood's return and he was transferred to Watford a year later.

This was not to be the start of a glorious new Tottenham era. And neither was it when Spurs returned to the new rebuilt Wembley in 2008 to beat Chelsea and lift the rebranded

Allan Nielsen stoops to conquer as he snatches the 1999 League Cup final winner

Carling Cup again. But on that day, the club in which I had invested so many emotions and spent most of my youthful days wishing and praying for, were winners. They were champions. The team that I had grown to associate with disappointment and despair had offered me my first taste of joy and hope. For the first time, I knew what it felt like to see my team hold aloft a trophy. And, like the scores of other fans of the same generation, it was a feeling that I never wanted to let go. I was then and forever would be a Tottenham Hotspur fan. And I'm forever grateful that, to this day, nothing about the club fails to amaze me.

39. Remembering Uncle Paul

STEFAN PAPE
Occupation: Sports/Film Journalist
Age: 23
Location: Paddington
Spurs fan since: Birth
All-time favourite player: Ledley King

Stefan is primarily a film critic, contributing to a variety of online publications. Also working in sports journalism, Stefan has had his articles published in *The Times* and *The Telegraph*, as well as having worked in his dream job; for *Hotspur* magazine.

ASK any Spurs fan how their love affair with the club first began and you'll no doubt hear of one particular moment. Whether this be a specific game, or merely a goal, there often appears to be that one pivotal point in time that fans highlight as being the catalyst that kick-started it all. I am, however, the exception to the rule, because I struggle to pinpoint a precise moment. Instead of recalling my very first game, or the first time I put on the Lilywhite shirt, instead I look to an entire childhood and an assertive family, who spoon-fed me the joys of Tottenham Hotspur, leading towards becoming the dedicated fan I am today.

As a toddler I used to fashion a sky blue Spurs baby-grow, given to me by my Uncle Paul on my very first birthday, leaving me little but no option to begin supporting this grand old club. The moment that my love affair began, you could argue, was my birth.

Spurs had been in the family for a number of decades, as my ancestors fell for the attractive football and congeniality of our squad under the great Bill Nicholson. And as time has progressed, despite the success lowering somewhat, the support has only continued to develop and augment. With a passionate and adoring fan in my mother, Joanna, and an ardent anorak in her brother, Paul, I can recall a childhood of complaining, frustration and incessant moaning, with names such as Dean Austin and Jason Dozzell bandied around in between expletives.

Yet by the age of six it was time to make up my own mind, and I was taken to my very first game by my mother, home to Norwich City on April 17, 1995, an experience I will never forget. You can never quite describe that first moment you walk up the concrete steps and emerge from the tunnel, only to find around 30 thousand other expectant and enthusiastic fans chanting, singing and conversing in unison, anticipating the team's arrival.

The deafening sound was louder than I could have ever expected. The vibrant yellow shirts of the away side more colourful than had ever appeared on the television. And then there were the players; the faces from the television, the names on the radio, the stickers on my wall. It all suddenly came to life, and there was an instantaneous understanding, there and then, that White Hart Lane and its inhabitants, were my home, and my family. Then when Teddy Sheringham scored the only goal of the game to earn us the three points, the eruption that followed has still never truly left me.

By that point I was well and truly sold on all things Tottenham Hotspur. Don't get me wrong, of course I soon joined the perturbed choir of fans, moaning unremittingly (particularly during the best forgotten Christian Gross era…), yet it had begun, I was Spurs.

My family were definitely my greatest influence. Going to a school full of Arsenal (can I say that word here?), Liverpool and Manchester United fans in North West London, I felt almost as though I had the responsibility of flying the lilywhite flag, making our presence known somewhat.

As an admirer of Eric Cantona, and being at such a tender and impressionable age, I'd be a liar if I said I was never tempted towards the glory and the success of Manchester United growing up, enviously looking on at my friends, celebrating their success with a degree of careless nonchalance, as I always imagined just how I would feel to see us lift the Premier League trophy. Yet I spurned approaches from peers, and remained faithful, adamant such success would soon arrive.

To be honest, I didn't actually have much choice as far as my family were concerned. I certainly felt that acceptance was a better option than potential abandonment (or being put up for adoption, perhaps) Having said that, I did have a second option available to me, in the form of Torquay United, who my Dad (having grown up there) supports, although I can assure you, his argument was certainly lacking in conviction.

Yet to avoid deciding between my parents, I had a majority rules scenario, as my uncle and auntie were also Spurs through and through; the former being an incredibly significant influence on me. Paul carried an incredible knowledge for Tottenham, and a passion to match. A self-declared anorak, he would compile Spurs-related lists, and often compare family pets, both past and present, to Spurs players from across the years. It's an obsessive trait I too possess, and, I hope, an adoration for the club equal to that of my uncle.

There is just something quite extraordinary about supporting Spurs, creating an

Teddy Sheringham, a predator and a perfectionist

apparent unity amongst fans. When someone walks besides you on the street wearing a badge bearing our famous cockerel, you often have to fight temptation to start speaking to them and discussing the side's prospects in the upcoming game.

There seems to be a constant desire to mention your affiliation with the club towards whoever will hear you out. We're proud, and we have every right to be. Rich in tradition and boasting some fine achievements and players over the years, we play the game as it should be. And despite a somewhat barren spell throughout my life, the club are as I write stronger than I have ever been fortunate enough to have seen, and I feel privileged to wear the colours and tell people that I support Spurs.

And it just makes you realise next time you go to White Hart Lane, nod your head to those sitting around you, those who share your passion and heartache, week in, week out – these people, too, have a story. They adore the club just as much as you do, following the side passionately; celebrating equally as much as you at that precise moment the ball hits the net, and sighing when conceding that pointless early goal.

These people have a moment too. They don't just support the club by accident, there will be a game, a goal, or similarly to my case, just a persuasive (yet entirely vindicated) family, but just like myself, they too caught the bug, and just like me, they haven't ever looked back either.

But I now look ahead, with hope and expectation. Things are on the up, and the glory days are not too far away. But I will forever think to my Uncle Paul as we progress. Sadly, he is no longer with us, having passed away in February 2011. But I feel his presence with every moment I watch the team about which he was so omniscient.

So as I look to the future without him in my life, I will forever be reminded of him through Spurs, dedicating every point we gain to his memory, proving that this is more than just a club, but a life membership. He bestowed such an honour upon me, and my younger brother and family members around me, and I almost feel a duty to continue such a fine legacy, and I would be privileged to have the same impact on the next generation of Spurs fans in my family.

And despite the fact my Mum has always apologised in advance if I ever ended up on the psychiatrist's chair as a result of supporting Spurs, it's fair to say I'm surviving. For now, at least.

BEN McALEER

Occupation: Freelance football journalist
Age: 23
Location: Winchester/London
Spurs fan since: 1997
All-time favourite player: David Ginola
Blog: http://thebeautifulgameweekly.blogspot.com
Website: http://www.tothelaneandback.com

Ben graduated with a degree in Media Communications, and is now breaking new ground in the competitive world of football journalism He founded the popular Glory Glory Tottenham Hotspur Facebook group (26,000-plus members) before concentrating on other pioneering Internet projects.

HINDSIGHT really is a wonderful thing. If it were a gift that was easily accessible, I'm sure a number of teams in the English Premier League would be in different circumstances today. Naturally, I fell in love with the mighty Tottenham Hotspur because of my father. He attended his first football game at the ripe old age of seven-years-old, and was lucky enough for it to have been the 1962 FA Cup final between Spurs and Burnley at Wembley.

As a young boy, the result didn't matter to him, just the thought of seeing the likes of captain Danny Blanchflower, Dave Mackay and Bobby Smith on the same pitch, following the instructions of the late, great Bill Nicholson, was enough to convince any football fan that the Lilywhites were playing the most attractive football in England at that moment.

However, it was the early strike of another Tottenham player on the day that caught my Dad's attention. He regularly reminds me whichever team scored the first goal on that afternoon in May, he would go on to support. Thankfully, it was Jimmy Greaves who struck for Spurs after just three minutes of the final as the North London giants went on to defeat the Clarets 3-1, with goals from Smith and Blanchflower enough to defend the prestigious cup.

This is where hindsight comes into effect, and my old man regularly proclaims how delighted he was that Greaves, now his life-long Spurs hero, scored the first goal on the afternoon and not Burnley's Jimmy Robson 47 minutes later.

Fast forward 49 years and his love for the club hasn't dimmed, if anything it's grown stronger with Tottenham's emphatic return to prominence.

But for me, time must be re-wound if we are to find my first game at White Hart Lane. I must confess, growing up I mainly followed Southampton, having lived in Winchester after a move from my birth place of Australia when I was four; they were seen as my local team.

I was at the naive age of nine when everything fell into place. My Dad took me – along with my my older brother and his friend, both avid Spurs fans – to the home League encounter against Sheffield Wednesday back in 1997.

It was my first trip to The Lane and, from when Jose Dominguez's strike hit the back of the net, my heart literally melted. Love at first sight is an over-rated expression used by secondary school children and their hour-long relationships, but for once the term couldn't have been more accurate on what was a surprisingly warm October afternoon. Goals from Chris Armstrong and my all-time favourite Spurs player David Ginola, who also had a special place in my late mother's heart, sealed a 3-2 win and helped begin my transition from a Saints fan to a Spurs one.

Back to the modern day and you will find a fully fledged Spurs fan, and season ticket holder, with the keyboard at my fingertips. A frequent visitor to White Hart Lane, and not one to turn down an away trip, and my love for the great North London side hasn't diminished one iota. I've witnessed the dark days of Juande Ramos and Christian Gross, the false dawn of Jacques Santini, the lasagne-gate reign of Martin Jol and, of course, the return to greatness under Harry Redknapp – and I wouldn't change any of it. Well, maybe the Ramos era, but he did land us a trophy,: the League Cup, with a vicory over Chelsea in the final and a day I will never forget.

Many have labelled the 2011-12 crop the best they have seen in the history of Spurs and you would be hard pressed to find any fan that disagrees. As I write, the current squad are playing with the beautiful attacking flair that has long been a Lilywhite tradition. Pacy wingers, the creative force in the middle with the Dave Mackayesque man supporting him, while the class on the front-line is evident for all too see. Many are indeed envious of the football currently witnessed at N17, and hopefully it will have been maintained by the time this Glory-Glory book is published.

My Dad continually drills into me the days gone by from Bill Nicholson's 16-year reign and Keith Burkinshaw's successful eight years at White Hart Lane, and he incessantly reminds me that the game that Redknapp has the first-team playing is in the tradition that the previous greats etched in the history of the club. The stories he tells me of Greaves, Mackay, Blanchflower, Perryman and Hoddle, to name but a few, is enough to convince me that Spurs really are the team to watch, and while I never got to see my Dad's heroes

Sandro, who brought Brazilian bite and fight to the Spurs midfield

in action, he assures me the likes of Parker, Modric and Bale are the closest I will get to seeing what his favourite players really were like back in the day.

And hearing the stories of yesterday's heroes compared to watching the players in the flesh today are both completely different in their own respects.

When the music booms out at White Hart Lane, the players emerge from the tunnel to a rapturous chorus of cheers and applause before the huddle to fire up the team and the fans. It is these small things that gets the Lane rocking and among the reasons I love Spurs so much. Whether it is a three o'clock kick-off or an evening game, nothing is more satisfying than seeing the players in white shirts go about their business in spectacular fashion and yet with an ease of effort that seems minimal.

Then, of course, comes the football. The scintillating array of talent that is on offer to the fans is almost second to none in comparison to a number of the Premier League heavyweights. The slick passing movement has left the Spurs faithful at times salivating, and with the 2011-12 season into its second half Tottenham have emerged as the most exciting team in the land.

For me, a picture making its way around the interweb of Sandro further depicts my love for the club. It is a still photograph of the Brazilian doing everything he can to keep the ball on the pitch after making a fantastic challenge on Chelsea defender Paulo Ferreira during the 1-1 draw with the Blues in December 2011. For all the flair and attacking prowess, the passion shown by the young midfielder in that passage of play signified all that is brilliant about Spurs as a club.

The same hunger for the game is relayed back to the fans who, both home and away, are one hundred per cent behind the players. And when the crowd at White Hart Lane is bellowing out the chants, the atmosphere rubs back off onto the players. It makes me proud to be a fan of this prestigious club when you see Bale marauding down the wing, Parker showcasing his art for a tremendous tackle or King turning out a 'Rolls Royce' of a performance despite his delicate knees.

Back to the beginning: How relieved I am that it was Jimmy Greaves who put the ball in the back of the net all those years ago and not Jimmy Robson for Burnley. Despite the ups and downs that can make every one of us require a Redknapp-style heart-op procedure, I wouldn't change it for one second. It is the passion of the fans, the hunger of the players, the technical flair and the moments of sheer genius that make Tottenham the most attractive team in the League as I sit here reminiscing at my keyboard.

Yes, those are the reasons why I love Spurs.

ANDREAS VOU
Occupation: Sports Journalist
Age: 22
Location: Barcelona/Larnaca/Southampton
Spurs fan since: Birth
All-time favourite player: Teddy Sheringham
Website: www.footballpanorama.wordpress.com

Andreas Vou was born and raised in Weston-super-Mare, moved to his ancestral home of Cyprus aged 14 and recently graduated from Southampton Solent University with a degree in Sports Journalism. Currently working for Catalunya's top sports newspaper *Mundo Deportivo* whilst also contributing to various other publications. He has been published in Greek, English and Spanish

IT wasn't a fun time growing up as a Spurs fan in the 90s. I had been passed down the burden from my Dad the same way he had from my Uncle Andrew. Of course, in their day they were lucky enough to witness the talents of Perryman, Hoddle, Archibald, Gascoigne and celebrated several FA Cup victories and a couple of UEFA Cup successes. Being too young to comprehend the 1991 FA Cup win, by the time I got to the age where I could actually process what was happening I was left with the likes of Justin Edinburgh, Jason Dozzell and Ramon Vega.

It really was the dullest period to be a Tottenham fan. We were the masters of mediocrity, pointlessly lingering in mid-table, neither challenging for a European place or even the odd relegation scrap to maintain consciousness.

Throughout my school life, I dreaded Monday mornings more than most as I would have to face incessant mocking of my team's shortcomings, primarily from the large number of questionable Manchester United fans.

My first taste of success came in 1999 in the form of the Worthington Cup against Leicester City when Allan Nielsen nodded in the rebound from Steffen Iversen's parried shot in the 94th minute. It would not have seemed like much of an achievement for one of the top sides at the time, but for my deprived generation it was the biggest feat we had ever experienced.

Despite our lack of continued success, I was well informed by the older Spurs fans in my family, as well as by old videos I had seen, of what a big club Spurs were and the great tradition associated with the club – yet I struggled to believe that I would ever live such glorious times based on what I was seeing at the time.

But the same way my family carried on the Spurs tradition through good and bad times in order to remind the next generation what the club was really about, so did certain players.

The one that made me identify most with the club was Teddy Sheringham. He personified everything I loved about football; first-time passing, superb vision, awareness, touch - all done with class and guile.

My first visit to White Hart Lane came in 2001 against Chelsea, the team we had failed to beat in our previous 19 attempts stretching over 14 years. Maybe I would be the lucky charm who could change our wretched form against our London rivals.

With the score at 1-1, Spurs were in the ascendency going in to the final fifteen minutes of the game when Jimmy Floyd Hasselbaink fell to the ground inside the box. Everyone inside the stadium saw the Dutchman kick the turf and upend himself with the nearest Spurs defender being at least a yard away yet the referee, after even consulting his linesman, awarded the penalty which Hasselbaink duly converted.

We were not done however, and thoroughly deserved by our display, Sheringham scored his second equalizer of the day to make it 2-2, his 100th Premier League goal. Yet just as it looked as though our hard work was to earn us a good point, with the last action of the game, Marcel Desailly found himself unmarked in the box and nodded in a 96th minute winner.

It was a cruel baptism for me, but still I won't ever forget the feeling of walking through the gate for the first time, the incredible atmosphere, the wave of emotions throughout the game and witnessing my hero Sheringham score two.

The nature of the result, however, summed up the 'Tottenham way' when I was growing up: one step forward, two steps back. Whether it was of our own out-doing or not, certain moments in our recent history always hampered any chance of returning to the glory days. Like Sheringham's decision to leave us in search of trophies at United in 1997, or Sol Campbell's infamous betrayal to join Arsenal in 2001, or even Pedro Mendes' ghost goal, when two extra points would have taken us into Europe that season. Instead, all we had to show were some great individual moments as opposed to trophies or high League finishes that would help us to build and progress.

In 2003 I moved with my family to Cyprus. Thanks to the massive Spurs following there and the help of foreign satellite that showed every Premier League game I was able to keep up with my team as much, if not more, as I did when I was in England.

My lifestyle had completely changed but Spurs' bad luck didn't. A year after we had lost

Spurs boss Harry Redknapp instilled the belief of doing things the right way

19 Premier League games, we looked to be on the right track by appointing the man who played a large part in making Lyon the biggest force in France, manager Jacques Santini. But even that optimism diminished no sooner than it had begun with the Frenchman quitting after just 13 League games due to disagreements with then sporting director Frank Arnesen.

The man Arnesen originaly signed as Santini's assistant, fellow Dutchman Martin Jol became manager, a move that turned out to be Spurs' rainbow after the storm. With his down to earth character off the field along with his attacking football philosophy on it, he proved to be the catalyst for Tottenham's return to the top.

In his second season in charge, we held the fourth and final Champions League position in the Premier League for more than six months only to be pipped at the last game of the seasons by the Gunners after the suspicious food-poisoning incident that left most of our first team in no condition to play the most important game of the club's recent history.

Carrying on the family tradition of passing the baton to the younger members, my brother and I did the same with our younger cousin in Cyprus, Antony, who within a few years under our guidance became a thoroughbred, borderline fanatic, Spurs supporter. I was proud to be the one to have taken him to his first game at White Hart Lane, the same way my cousin George did with me in 2001. Similar to my first visit to the Lane, it was a cruel induction. A 0-1 defeat to the most dire team you could ever wish to see live, Stoke City. Our respective first games at the Lane were seemingly tests of faith: take the easy way out early on or endure struggle to achieve success. Our devotion to the latter has more than paid off.

It's memories like those that molded the attitude I now have about Tottenham. While at times it can be the most stressful job in the world, it has taught me and the thousands of other Spurs fans of my generation that patience pays off and allows us to cherish what we have become today as the past was so tedious.

In the last six seasons we have achieved fifth place on three occasions, fourth place in 2010 and reached the quarter finals of the Champions League. After continuous support from the fans, fulfilled potential of many of our players and heroic work from our chairman Daniel Levy we are back where we want to be, competing amongst the top teams both at home and abroad.

"You have to know the past to understand the present." The perfect quote to characterize a Spurs fan of my age. I see it as a blessing that we went through fruitless times so we can fully appreciate our current status, understanding our goals rather than be over-demanding and form a greedy mentality like many of our rival fans have.

In the past we had quality players like Ginola and Klinsmann but they were largely in and around average Tottenham sides. We are fortunate to see players of that class all in the same starting line-up: Modric, Bale, Van der Vaart alongside other very good players under the guidance of one the best managers in our history. I must admit that I was apprehensive about Harry Redknapp's appointment but his character was perfect for us at the time. Our two consecutive fifth-place finishes in 2006 and 2007 made us feel as though we were owed a place in the Champions League. Harry's grounded approach towards the media, fans and players gave out the feeling of confidence with realism rather than radical promises. He instilled the belief of doing things the right way over time, rather than rushing and doing things wrong. Exactly 24 months later, we beat the defending European Champions Inter Milan 3-1.

If history is to serve as a guide, as it so often does, we must follow the lessons we have learnt over the years to reach the next level.

Be grateful, be patient and keep the faith

SAM ROOKE
Occupation: Freelance Journalist
Age: 22
Location: London via Sydney
Spurs fan since: 2005
All-time favourite player: Dimitar Berbatov

Sam has been bitten so hard by the Spurs bug that he has moved to London from Sydney to follow a career as a sports journalist. He grew up in Australia with no knowledge of "soccer" until stumbling on TV pictures of a team in white. He's quickly caught up with his history, and here's the proof:

COME with me Down Under to discover how the spirit of Spurs travelled 10,500 miles to capture me, heart and soul. My story starts with an idle moment flicking through the television channels and coming across a game of soccer, which is what I called the sport then.

I don't really know why I was watching it. Growing up in Sydney, football was just not on the radar. The success of the national team would eventually bring prominence, but in 2005 it was still the ugly duckling of Australian sports. My Dad had been a semi-professional footballer in Australia, but still it held no interest for me.

I could have switched it off immediately, but something about the colours stayed my hand on the remote-control. The deep green of the pitch was nothing like the grass I played rugby on, the huge yellow boards running right around the stadium telling me that 'To Dare is to Do' and the white shirts were all attractive to me.

After a moment, I heard the commentator say that the team in white were about to beat the team in blue, something that had not happened in my lifetime. I suddenly felt a small connection and watched the rest of the match.

I honestly felt anxiety as I watched the time inexorably tick away. The reactions of the fans, manager and players at full time left an indelible mark on me. I just didn't know it yet.

About a year later, I had found another game, a replay. The same team in white, this time playing a team in claret and blue. It was already 2-1 so I thought it would be worth watching. When Dimitar Berabatov scored his free kick in that epic 4-3 I was hooked.

The casual brilliance and arrogance to score that goal was the first part of football that I knew to be different to other sports. This was something I hadn't seen before and I needed to see more of it. Much more.

I have since gone back and watched both the Chelsea 2-1 and the West Ham game many times. They hold a unique place for me, part of my Tottenham education. It was the brilliant Bulgarian who is the most to thank (or to blame?) for my affliction. The one we all suffer from.

His goal against Charlton, so hard to find on YouTube, was breathtaking. The flick and turn to leave the defender, the drop of the shoulder to lose another and the simple finish showed me a grace and control that I knew to be special. His was a special blend of arrogance and class that shone like a beacon, even to one so unenlightened as me.

From those beginnings, I began reading all I could find about this club and watching the classic moments on the internet, I was already converted. Tony Parks in the UEFA cup, the Gascoigne free kick, Klinsmann's four against Wimbledon and the majestic dive after his first goal. Each of these moments built up to my own pieces of Tottenham history.

Claiming the Carling Cup under Juande Ramos and then the relegation scare before Harry Redknapp's arrival cemented my allegiance. That night in Manchester and those nights in Milan. To experience so many emotions; joy and despair, rage and elation all in just 90 minutes was special.

After Berbatov there was Bale. The free kick against Arsenal and the goal against Fulham showed that this kid, and – about my age – he was just a kid, was special. Of course we all know that now. Then there was Modric. His performance in an otherwise nondescript 3-1 against Stoke is one of my most cherished footballing memories. Everything that I understand football to be was on display that night.

There was Robbo's goal against Watford and Ledley's tackle on Robben. Watching other teams play may have been enjoyable, but it was nothing like watching Spurs. I have never been able to really explain it, but I think that's part of it. You don't choose your team. In a strange way, you just sort of realise that they have always been your team. That's why the history matters so much.

I certainly never saw the Double Team, but I know they were so special because they are a part of the club that is a part of me. I feel like it's just a memory from long ago. For most fans, I'm sure that's a familiar feeling. For me though, joining so recently, even players like Ginola, Klinsmann, Gazza; I never saw them play, but I love them for what I know they did and I know that I would have loved them if I'd had the chance.

Gradually, I uncovered a world of Tottenham fans that I had never realised existed. I used to get up between two and five in the morning to watch Spurs games, feeling like I was part of something unique.

Now in London, I recently went to my first away game and realised that I am not alone.

Dimitar Berbatov, whose skill and invention caught an imagination Down Under

I and hundreds of kindred spirits made a long train ride to stand in the rain and sing and shout and watch our team lose. Despite that, it was a magnificent experience that I hope to be the first of many such trips.

I have never known other football fans to speak with such passion about why they follow their club. We speak, all of us, about a commitment to playing the right way; about an attitude, summed up by a few men that were so vital in the history of Tottenham Hotspur. There's Bill Nicholson and Danny Blanchflower and then there's that famous photo of Dave Mackay holding Billy Bremner by the collar. I don't think I know anyone I haven't shown it to.

I was told to write here about why I am a Tottenham fan. I honestly feel like asking why anyone would ever ask such a question. How could you not be?

The contagion has brought me 10,500 miles to England to follow a career as a football journalist, with an eye on the game in general but with feelings and passion for Spurs in particular. I am a long way from home … yet, with White Hart Lane so close, I somehow *feel* at home.

43. Anderton, my poster hero

BRIAN Mc LAUGHLIN

Occupation: Student
Age: 21
Location: Dublin via Letterkenny
Spurs fan since: 1990
All-time favourite player: Darren Anderton

Brian is studying International Relations at Dublin City University. He enjoys all things Tottenham, and is just laying the foundations to what he hopes will be long experience writing about the Spurs club he discovered when he was an eight-year-old schoolboy in Ireland.

I WAS always going to be a Tottenham Hotspur fan from birth. My Dad, Charlie, was a Spurs man so I would grow up to be a Spurs man. Admittedly, I never really took much interest in the games or the results until I was a little older. Perhaps it was just as well, as when I was growing up it was the 90s – not exactly our Glory, Glory years! Of course, as I was to find out, it's easier to get in than it is to get out. I know many Spurs fans will testify to this; following Spurs can result in mood swings, from the most joyous of games to the worst of the worst, and Spurs really have produced some of the worst through the years.

One Saturday afternoon Dad announced that we were going to the pub to watch Spurs play Leicester in the Worthington Cup Final at Wembley. My brother and I didn't really pay much heed to be honest; we were just excited at the prospect of going to the pub with all of the grown-ups. For an eight year old the pub means only one thing – fizzy drinks! So we were only too happy to go, of course. We piled into our Rover 45 and drove down to the local. The excitement was gradually building. I was going into the unknown really; I felt like the luckiest kid in the world because I was getting to go to the pub with my Dad to watch football. I would get to brag about this in school for the next week. "I was in a pub. Watching football. With my Dad". As you can gather, Dad is very special in my life.

When we got our drinks, we watched the game on the big screen projector. I was amazed; firstly, I'd never seen a television so big! I'd also never seen so many football fans in the one place, certainly never as many Tottenham fans in one room. I was used to it being just me and my Dad and my brother, but now there were at least twenty others, and to an eight year old like me, I might have just as well been in Wembley! One thing that really stands out in my memory is a pre-match advert for Carling. It featured a "Middle-Ages" type scene where a bunch of men start playing football with a can in the street when suddenly one of the

Darren 'Sick Note' Anderton, for whom opponents had a healthy respect

spectators yells "Offside!" The spectator turns to him and asks "What's offside?" and the reply was a shrug of the shoulders. I thought this was hilarious at the time.

The game was amazing to my eight year old eyes. The grass was so green on the screen, our shirts were so white and theirs were so blue. My Dad and the other men around were getting really worked up, shouting at the screen. It was quite a scrappy game and we had Justin Edinburgh sent off (some would say after some theatrics from one Mr. R. Savage). My brother and I took it in our stride. I don't really think that we were fully aware that it was the cup final, but I was gradually getting more and more involved. I began to try to follow the game as it wore on and I could tell that it was going to come right down to the end.

I remember the goal so clearly. Stefan Freund bore down the right wing and he rifled it goalwards. The keeper parried into the path of Allan Nielsen's head. Back of the net! The pub went mad. It seemed to my brother and I that the world had just exploded. Everybody was shouting and screaming and jumping up and down. To tell you the truth, we were a little overwhelmed by it all. We celebrated too, of course, because we wanted to fit in.

It seemed like the entire stadium was full of Spurs fans celebrating, bonded by going 1-0 in the lead towards the end of a cup final. Something had clicked inside me. There was something right about Tottenham. I didn't know the history, I didn't know many of the players, I didn't know where we played and I didn't even know where Tottenham was, but none of that mattered. I was attracted to the win (you may label me a glory hunter if you wish) and I was attracted to Spurs. After the match I had swimming lessons in the local pool, and I was still hyped up from the excitement of the match. I was boasting to everyone I met, asking them if they saw the game and if they knew Spurs were cup winners. One of the other kids tried to put a dampener on things by saying the goal was offside but it mattered not one jot to me. I should have shrugged and asked as in the TV advertisement, "What's offside?"

I was elated by the victory and I realised school the following week would be even better. I knew none of the others would laugh when I said I supported Spurs, because we were Cup Champions. I could get used to that. Later on that season, my Dad went to White Hart Lane for a game and brought back a load of Spurs stuff; posters, stationary, wallpaper and bed covers. Needless to say the room got a swift redecoration.

Among the treasures brought back by Dad was a Darren Anderton poster, and that made me decide that Darren would be my favourite player. It's strange the little things that motivate kids to pick their hero. I picked a good one though, guided by my Dad's choice of poster and excellent judgment. I still use the Tottenham Hotspur pencil case he picked up that day too; I always feel proud when I take it out of my bag at university!

That has led me to where I am today; 21 years old and as Spurs mad as ever. Sadly I don't get over to games as much as I'd like to, though I have picked two good ones in the past: the 4-2 v Bolton Wanderers where Keane scored two, got sent off and Berbatov was man of the match because of a sterling lone performance up front. The second was Harry's first game in charge, and I think we all know how that one went and the wonderful adventure since.

DAVID NORDLINGER
Occupation: Student at Duke University, USA
Age: 21
Location: North Carolina
Spurs fan since: 1998
All-time favourite player: Darren Anderton

David was born in Washington DC in 1990, and moved with his lawyer father to London in 1992 and lived there until 2009. He attended Westminster School before taking a place at the highly regarded Duke University to read Political Science and Arabic.

BY rights, I should be a Chelsea fan. When I was brought over from the United States as a young kid, I was given all the necessary tools to become a Chelsea supporter. I lived in West London, I attended primary school at the start of the Zola heyday, I even went to a match at Stamford Bridge. And yet somehow I don't support Chelsea. I am not saying it is unique for a West Londoner to support a team other than Chelsea. In fact there are a large number of West Londoners who don't support Chelsea. I am merely hinting that my love for Tottenham was not set in stone from the day I moved to London

Like most young children without a football-supporting father, I was drawn to the best clubs of the day. I was a fan of Gianfranco Zola, and Vialli because I thought it was funny that a manager would throw himself on to play. Unfortunately, I was a little bit taken with Arsenal – they played Tottenham's style of football so well in the first years of Wenger's reign.

After the 1998 world cup, I had decided that it was time to find myself a club. Naturally I was drawn to Chelsea and Arsenal; I didn't want to follow a team outside of London for obvious reasons. Therefore my father bought tickets to Wimbledon-Arsenal, and we made the trek out to Selhurst Park. However, at the match I found myself cheering for The Dons – I have always had a soft spot for underdogs. I was ecstatic when Wimbledon scored a blatant handball goal to beat Arsenal at the death. Yet, I couldn't seriously follow Wimbledon – their style of football was hardly a thing of beauty.

And then there was Tottenham. I did not know much about the club except that my best friend was always resigned to the team giving away leads. His father was, and still is, a

Spurs season-ticket holder, and so my mate would go to the Lane for every home match. I wasn't especially jealous of my friend back then – let's face it, the 1997-1998 season wasn't exactly a throwback to 1961. Yet, I loved the atmosphere generated at football grounds and I wished I could have gone to a match every fortnight. Then, as a birthday present, my friend invited me to the Liverpool match on December 5 1998.

When I got the invite I was excited: I always wanted to watch Liverpool play. However, I started to get a little bit more interested in Tottenham. Who were they? Arsenal's rivals: that sounded good. A team with Jewish history: sounded even better. The best team since the early 1960s: well I sort of missed the boat on that front. Who played for them? David Ginola: stylish. Sol Campbell: quality. Darren Anderton: injured. Ruel Fox: who? With my limited knowledge I summed up Tottenham as a mid-table team with a handful of quality players and loyal fans, like my friend – a team that would cause me more heartache than joy.

On the day, I met my friend and his father at Liverpool Street Station (which confused me, because Tottenham Court Road seemed more apt), and we caught the overground to White Hart Lane. The train ride seemed interminable, and I could not get over the fact that most Spurs fans were wearing shirts that promoted my printer. Yet, I could feel genuine excitement, tempered by a bit of apprehension, throughout the train carriage. Somehow this was different to the build up I had experienced before the Chelsea and Arsenal matches. For the first time in my life I was infected by pre-match vibrancy.

As the match started I could feel myself being drawn to Tottenham. Every time Ginola received the ball I expected a majestic run, whenever Anderton ran I wanted a pinpoint cross. Yet, as the minutes dragged on without a goal being scored, my patience was tested. Until a goal was scored, there was a still a way out of supporting Spurs. Ruel Fox scored the first goal, but surprisingly I was not completely sold on Tottenham. I clapped and smiled, but something was still holding me back from selling myself to the club.

Unfortunately, that exit road was finally blocked off by a brilliant Jamie Carragher goal. The ball was delivered into the box, beckoning Armstrong to apply the finishing touch. Carragher, leaving nothing to chance, applied the finishing touch himself, with horrendous or hilarious results, depending on your view. Sliding in ahead of Armstrong he guided the ball past a despairing David James, into the bottom corner. If a striker had scored it, the goal would have been labelled a clinical finish; however, because Carragher scored, it will just go down as the first in a string of own goals for the Liverpudlian.

As the goal went in, I remember jumping in the air in ecstasy before breaking down into uncontrollable laughter. I was hooked. I spent the rest of the match biting my nails; experiencing the first of many Tottenham attempts to grasp defeat from the jaws of victory. The Patrick Berger free kick goal sparked a thirty-minute barrage on the Tottenham goal that brought the rollercoaster emotions that every fan sadistically enjoys. Every ball into

Ruel Fox, who scored the first Spurs goal witnessed by David Nordlinger

the box brought a heart attack, which was temporarily eased with each clearance – until we realized that the clearance went straight to the feet of a Liverpool player ensuring the painful cycle.

After the match, I avidly followed Tottenham's progress for the remainder of the season. Unfortunately, it was at this point when I realized that most of my friends were Arsenal supporters – and there was not much I could say when they came second and we finished twelfth, behind the likes of Derby and Leicester. Yet, ironically this misfortune strengthened my support for the club.

Honestly, I never believed that Tottenham could come close to replicating the past glories. However, there is something wrong when one feels great anger at a loss or a draw, but little joy with a win.

Tottenham has the perfect balance. As a large club, with a great history, that specialises in exciting football we are able to enjoy the game played the right way. We might not have won much compared to the likes of United and Liverpool, but there can be no doubt that if the title was awarded to the team that played the most exciting games we would win every year.

Now, back home and studying in the United States, my attention to all things Tottenham is no less; if anything, sharpened and more in focus thanks to the all-embracing satellite coverage of the Premier League. And from here on the other side of the Pond, it looks as if the Glory-Glory years could be on their way back for Spurs. I am so glad I did not do the obvious and select Chelsea as my club. COYS.

Declan Olley

Occupation: Journalism Student
Age: 18
Location: Kent University
Spurs fan since: 1998
All-time favourite player: Luka Modric
Websites: www.declanolley.wordpress.com
www.notpremierleagueprovenp0dcast.blogspot.com

Declan is an aspiring and creative sports journalist. With a pen, he writes about Spurs and European football. With a microphone, he is involved in Not Premier League Proven, a podcast run by six Kent journalism students available on iTunes.

> *"And for you sir?" asked the Italian waiter.*
> *"What," I replied, "do you recommend?"*
> *"It has to be the dish of the day, sir ... lasagne ..."*

IT all comes back to me now like a bad dream. Standing in the away end at Upton Park slowly realising that all of the points Martin Jol's Tottenham had amassed since August had amounted to absolutely nothing. A magnificent season wasted.

But looking back on that miserable day in the East End it was to be the start of my love affair with Tottenham Hotspur.

It had been a rollercoaster season so far in the Premier League for Spurs. There was the 1-1 draw at Old Trafford which should have been 2-1, but I'm sure you all know about that. Robbie Keane's brace that saw Tottenham grab a vital 3-2 victory over Blackburn at home. And of course, that famous image of Martin Jol going head-to-head with Arsene Wenger in the last ever North London Derby at Highbury.

Tottenham were going into the last match of the season in a position they had never been in before: in fourth place and one point ahead of the arch enemy – the Woolwich Nomads. It meant that all Spurs needed to do in the 38th and final game of the 2005/2006 season was to equal or better Arsenal's result to stay above the Gunners and reach the Holy Grail – the Champions League.

In the days leading up to the game, public opinion appeared to be with the red side of North London. Some said it was because Arsenal were playing against 'a nothing-to-play-for' Wigan Athletic side, and it was also their last ever game at Highbury, so both the points and the fortune were with them. Others meanwhile, said that Tottenham would simply crumble under the pressure at Upton Park and meet a West Ham team wanting to get one over on their London rivals.

But no one could have expected what was to come on May 6 2006.

The night before the game I remembered one moment my Dad always told me about – the 1984 UEFA Cup win against Anderlecht. I found the game on Youtube before I went to sleep and watched the glory unfold before my eyes. That was it; I wanted to be part of a European adventure with Spurs.

During my sleep that night I can still vividly recount the dream inspired by that video. I had envisaged myself in the upper echelons of the Camp Nou watching Robbie Keane and company take on the best club side in the world. Surely if the Spurs players dreamed of this too then a win against a mid-table side with one eye on the FA Cup final a week later, was a formality.

I awoke earlier than usual, but upon getting out of bed I felt something I had never felt before going to a football match – nerves. Was this normal? Was I becoming too hung up on Spurs? It was indeed the first signs of my 'close relationship' with the club, but as a 13 year-old I was not to know that.

Time passed quickly after I got up and it was soon that we were to leave. My Dad had been sporting the famous North London Branch Barcelona supporter's club shirt all morning. The shirt was in support of our friends from Cataluña, who we so desperately needed to beat Arsenal in the Champions League final, because if the Gunners won the game then they could be given a 2006/2007 Champions League place at our expense.

But there was more to that shirt than rivalry. It was the humour that I particularly enjoyed; the Barcelona badge had the Spurs cockerel embedded into it and the club abbreviation FCB had been turned into THFCB. That's what I enjoyed about Tottenham – the fans knew how to have a laugh.

Laughing though was not on the agenda when we switched over to Sky Sports News during our lunch. Running across the bottom of the screen were the words "Tottenham request game against West Ham to be postponed" . We couldn't believe it. What were we reading? What was going on?

Then like all good stories, it developed. The team had been staying overnight in the Marriot Hotel in Canary Wharf, and the majority of the squad had contracted food poisoning, which was later found to be caused by lasagne. Subsequently, Tottenham wanted the game to be postponed. It has gone down in the annals as 'Lasagnegate'.

Controversy ensued. Only a club like Tottenham could be involved in something like this, but how I loved feeling a part of the drama. I was even more convinced Tottenham had everything I wanted from football, and I wouldn't be disappointed in the many years to come because drama has never been in short supply.

Despite the doubts the game was to go ahead, and we would have to get a move on. The car journey was anxious to say the least, but my nerves were turning to excitement. And our arrival at Upton Park only reinforced the change in feelings. Fear had crept into me though as we wandered through the hordes of Hammers fans. The stories of the Inter City Firm and the violence of Green Street gave me reason to be aware of what was around me, despite my age. Reaching the away end was a relief. I felt at home.

The conversations along the concourses were all about the same subject: food poisoning. Surely it wouldn't affect the players that much? Surely a place in the Champions League would make the players forget about the illness? Then the team news was announced. No Ledley King, no Jermaine Jenas and Danny Murphy was on the bench.

Walking up the stairs to our seats the nerves returned, but I couldn't understand the optimism amongst some of the Spurs fans. Balloons were being thrown all over the place – was I missing something, had Spurs already achieved fourth place? The first 10 minutes of the match certainly dispelled that optimism.

Tottenham had begun sluggishly, West Ham went 1-0 up through a fine goal by Carl Fletcher and Arsenal had gone 1-0 up. But drama was the order of the day and so news of Wigan getting a quick-fire equaliser shouldn't have been a surprise.

The initial storm was weathered by Spurs and they began to settle into the game, yet there was one hell of a storm cooking up at Highbury – Arsenal had gone behind. The Spurs fans faces were no longer a sign of worry and when Jermaine Defoe equalised for Tottenham, it was pandemonium.

In a matter of seconds that was all over. Thierry Henry had levelled the scores back at Highbury and the worry was once again etched on the Spurs fans faces. The half-time whistle was a welcome relief to a frantic first 45 minutes, but as it stood, Spurs would finish fourth.

The second half was much like the first. In the opening 10 minutes Tottenham conceded a penalty, only for old boy Teddy Sheringham to be denied by Paul Robinson. The reaction of the Spurs fans was priceless as they chanted "You're Spurs, and you know you are!" at the ex-Lane man. Then the chants were coming from the Upton Park faithful: "Arsenal, Arsenal, Arsenal". They had gone 3-2 up. I couldn't believe it – West Ham fans cheering for another London team. I knew that they loved to hate Tottenham but that was a step too far. Another enemy to add to the list, and another reason for my loyalty to be given to Spurs. It was an uphill task for Tottenham, and it got even bigger when Thierry Henry got his hat-trick to put Arsenal 4-2 up. Attack was the only option for Spurs, but with food poisoning taking its toll and ideas lacking West Ham delivered the knockout blow on the 80th minute. A wonderful Yossi Benayoun goal gave the Hammers a 2-1 lead and saw the red side of North London steal fourth place.

Lane legend Ledley King, one of the 'Lasagnegate' victims

For the first time since I began watching Spurs in 2000 a sense of dejection and frustration grabbed me. Walking out of the stadium I took a glance at the Bobby Moore Upper stand and saw the West Ham fans showcasing us the very worst of sign language. It only fuelled my anger.

The journey home was a time of quiet calm and reflection though. I could see the hurt in my Dad's eyes; all those years since that famous night in 1984 he had been waiting for Spurs to dine at Europe's elite table. But for myself, I was simply spurred on (no pun intended). I learned from the experience that supporting Tottenham would be full of the best highs and the worst lows. I knew we would be a perfect match.

Sitting in an Italian cafe three and half years later, I decided upon that lasagne. Not because the waiter had recommended it but because it symbolised how far my love affair with Tottenham had taken me – to the San Siro in the Champions League.

The disappointment that was to come that evening was a little different to the one on May 6 2006, but the love still remained, and does so still to this day ... and far beyond.

SWC THE ASSOCIATE MEMBERS

WE members of the Spurs Writers' Club need the support and interest of readers if our project is to grow beyond this first book. My old mate Jimmy Greaves, who was quite impressive in a Tottenham shirt, beautifully put me in my place when I told him I was forming a Spurs Writers' Club. 'Wouldn't it be more sensible,' he said, straight faced, 'to form a Spurs Readers' club?'

What we are hoping to do is build up a following of Associate Members, people who support and encourage us by buying our books at discounted prices. If you have not yet registered as an Associate Member, please contact me by email at unclenorman@ normangillerbooks.co.uk or get in touch through any of our Members featured in this book.

When I first came up with the idea, there were cynics on line who dismissed it as a scam. But actually it is a scheme rather than a scam. Our club consists of a democratic collective of writers who will be sharing the overheads so that nobody gets badly burned (I have the scars to prove that publishing ventures can scorch you if you get the planning wrong).

None of us will get rich with the books, but we will have the satisfaction of chronicling the events at Tottenham, the club that makes our heart beat faster and occupies hours or our thinking, talking and dreaming time.

We have ambitious plans provided we get this launch book to kick us off in style. There are dozens of ideas on the drawing board, including an in-depth look at the Harry Redknapp years at The Lane. Now there's a best seller if ever I smelt one.

Associate Members will be involved in future books. We will be asking them to contribute views and opinions on set subjects about Spurs, their players, achievements, records and memorable matches and moments.

The Big Plan is to have a library of Spurs Writers' Club books covering all aspects of the Tottenham Hotspur history, but we cannot do it without readers. Please encourage other Spurs supporters to become Associate Members and join in the Great Publishing Adventure.

On the following page there is a roll call of the first Associate Members to pledge their support before a book had been published. We hope YOU will join them in our next Spurs Writers' Club venture. COYS.

Matt Boxall (Hertfordshire)

Tom Boxall (Hertfordshire)

Richard Butterworth (London E3)

Dennis Cooper (Kent)

Rodney Cooper (Gwynedd, Wales)

Norman Davies (Kent)

Deepak Arora (London W1)

Neil Fisher (Hampshire)

Nicole Forder (Kent)

Stuart Field (Warwickshire)

Tim Franey (South London)

Steve Grubb (Dunfermline)

Stephen Hawkins (Cornwall)

Sandra Holmes (Northern Ireland)

Paul Hunt (Essex)

Matt Hutchison (Kent)

Andy Iles (Hertfordshire)

Will Irwin (West Sussex)

Kathryn Jones (Hertfordshire)

Mandy Kilpatrick (Surrey)

Paul Knox (London W4)

Michael Lambert (Hertfordshire)

Alan Langley (Canada)

Ronnie Lawrence (Essex)

Amanda Lovatt (Hertfordshire)

Dan Magner (East Sussex)

Pauline Metcalfe (Tyne & Wear)

Pauline Molyneux (Cheshire)

Joop Noordman (Holland)

Raymond Parker (Northern Ireland)

Tony Poole (Lower Clapton Hackney)

Colin Raffell (Devonshire)

Tom Rimmer (Bucks)

Adele Ryntjes (Middlesex)

Alan Scopp (Vienna)

Matthew Selby (Essex)

Trevor Skinner (Kent)

Andy Spurrier (Devonshire)

Luigi Sterlini (North London)

Julia Stone (Hertfordshire)

Gareth Thomas (Maryland, USA)

Roy van Dijk (Holland)

Henri van der Veen (Holland)

Joost van Leeuwen (Holland)

Clive Walters (Watford)

Garry Walters (Middlesex)

Josephine Watson (Essex)

Ian Wilson (Northern Ireland)

Gijs Zandbergen (Holland)